PEAK
Performance!!

MERGING SPIRITUALITY & SUCCESS PRINCIPLES

Alan Sullivan

SULLIVAN WORLD PUBLISHING

MW00488991

Copyright © 2016 by Alan Sullivan.

All rights reserved. No part of this publication may be reproduced, distributed or transmitted in any form or by any means, including photocopying, recording, or other electronic or mechanical methods, without the prior written permission of the publisher, except in the case of brief quotations embodied in critical reviews and certain other noncommercial uses permitted by copyright law. For permission requests, write to the publisher at the address below.

Author: Alan Sullivan
Publisher: Sullivan World
www.sullivanworld.com
E-mail: alan@sullivanworld.com
Peak Performance website: www.capdevt.com

Ordering Information:
Discounts are available on quantity purchases. For details, contact the publisher by e-mail.

Peak Performance!! Merging Spirituality and Success Principles, Alan Sullivan
Paperback black & white version, 1st Edition.
ISBN: 978-0-9935855-1-7

Contents

Preface

It is rare to find both *spirituality* and *success* covered in one book. And, although the importance of spirituality to wellbeing and success has been recognized in research studies, it appears to have been highly underrated. It is hoped, then, that this book will help to bridge the gap, so that you can both *awaken* and *achieve* greatly, and live an outstanding life on your own terms.

There is a place for cave-based meditators whose sole focus is on awakening and perhaps raising world consciousness, but this book is aimed at people who are interested in utilizing their spiritual wellbeing as a foundational springboard for worldly success. In absorbing spiritual principles, you can choose to live more boldly, and your life's adventures will be more colorful for the mystery and surprises.

In merging spiritual and success principles, we advocate full engagement in the world. A good spiritual grounding will make you wiser, relatively fearless, more self-accepting, and increase your capacity for giving and receiving the best in life. You may well find though, that your idea of what "the best" is changes, and that many things no longer bother you, leading to both a change in your priorities and more effective resolution of issues arising.

Indeed, in considering spirituality first, you can ensure that your life mission and goals are grounded in your true self. You can avoid the stress of chasing things that ultimately wouldn't serve you or others well, and choose an effective mission that embraces both worldly success goals and your spiritual wellbeing.

While the scope of this book mainly concerns spirituality and worldly success, it touches on broader aspects of wellbeing and mood-management such as sleep, diet, exercise and the external environment. In addition, this book is not religious, and is suitable for anyone irrespective of their faith. This book provides *unique visual content* that is not available anywhere else, to help you make the shift from an ego-led life to an awakened one.

While you may find some "old wine in new bottles," I trust that you will find a lot of life-enhancing, integrative and new insights that will help you to see your life in a new and refreshing perspective, and help you to live a truly outstanding life! Onwards and upwards!

Alan Sullivan MSc, MBA

i

This book is dedicated to my family

To thine own self be true.

— William Shakespeare, Hamlet

Who are you and why are you here?

Our lives can often be frenetic and complex, related to the various roles that we play and the degree of fit and overlap between them. If we feel that we are being pulled in different directions or have too many obligations or insufficient time to meet deadlines, then the conditions of our life situation can cause us stress. There is a danger, that if we can't see the "Big Picture" of how best to live authentically, we may get trapped in a life not of our liking. Life can then be likened to a "Hamster Wheel" where people are very busy and stressed, yet achieving little of real meaning. Or, we may find that our ladder (of purpose) has been leaning against the wrong wall. Our lives need to be authentic, fulfilling and light, with a sense of joy, rather than superficial, frustrating and heavy with fleeting glimpses of happiness.

The emphasis of this book, is on having, or *deliberately manifesting*, an outstanding life, fully immersed in the flow of life and all that it has to offer. In order for this to happen, and as a starting point, it's important that we have a clear idea of who we are and what our purpose is, and this will guide us in how we show up in the world. In examining our roots, beginnings and original source, we are inevitably and unavoidably drawn into considering the mysteries of the universe and spirituality.

Indeed, we are advocating for a more spirit-led approach to creating manifestations in our lives, while fully recognizing the role of the occasionally neurotic human ego. This is not a *new age* book. It is not about intangible airy fairy notions drawn out of thin air that may generate doubt, skepticism and mistrust of the message. We know that we live in a huge, miraculous, mysterious, incredulous universe of which our understanding as human beings is rather limited. This limited understanding necessitates that we make some assumptions about this universe and our place in it. As far as possible, such assumptions need to be based on scientific evidence and deductive reasoning as befitting our modern era.

This book is organized in 3 parts. Part 1 develops the "RAFTS Map" **R**esults, **A**ctions, **F**eelings, **T**houghts and **S**tate concerning the process of manifesting meaningful results in our lives. Sub-Maps are introduced that help to ensure that our choices are grounded in our authentic selves, leading to harmony and fulfillment. Part 2 is built upon the acronym FLAGS: **F**reedom, **L**ove, **A**dventures, **G**ratitude and **S**ervice that can be considered as worthy personal "values" to live by, although of course everyone is free to choose values that feel personally congruent for them. Freedom and love go hand in hand, or one could say form two sides of the same coin – it is only by becoming really free that the creative energy of the universe and love can flow through us unimpeded. If freedom and love provide the juice and zest for life, then our adventures and gratitude for our manifestations provide the fruits of fulfillment. Adventures and gratitude also go together like two sides of the same coin. Adventures provide us with experiences, moments, memories and meaning, adding to our store of things to be grateful for. Service refers to adopting a helpful attitude towards others and our planet and the wider environment based on healthy desires and not out of obligation or fear. Living from service and the other values determines our legacy – how deeply we have been a force of good in the world for others as well as ourselves. Part 3 is based on the acronym HIVE: **H**abits, **I**magination, **V**alues and **E**xpression. Our daily habits and use of our imaginations are major determinants of successful manifestations while our values or needs determine our choices and their expression into the world.

In this introduction, we look at some important questions about *whom we are* and *why we are here* on Planet Earth as a prelude to the main content of this book which concerns how we can make our time on Earth the most beneficial for ourselves and others.

Who are you?

"Who am I?" is an interesting question that you may have asked as a small child and then promptly forgotten about as there was no simple answer to this enduring mystery of self. In the absence of any verifiable information, perhaps the easiest way to approach this question is to go back in time in your mind at a very fast rate. Try, for example, to run life on Planet Earth backwards in your mind at a rate of 100 years per second.

How well you do this exercise depends a bit on some historical knowledge and any interests you may have in important religious luminaries. Just knowing, for example, the time of the Ministry of Jesus 2,000 years ago, (20 seconds back in time at 100 years per second), and the Buddha another 600 years or 6 seconds in time at the same rate and imagining man-made infrastructure returning to forest, grassland and desert will get you on your way. In the 20 seconds or so between today and Anno Domini 1 as you go back in time the Earth's population has shrank from around 7 billion to 200 million. Just a little more time and you will see the first human beings who roamed this planet. You may start to wonder if you, (and everyone else), are intimately related to these first human beings. Our recognizable ancestors, with the arising of the spoken word, independent thought (and ego), commenced perhaps 50,000 to 60,000 years ago – around 10 minutes back in time at 100 years per second. Yet, our ancestral roots may well go back millions of years and we may have evolved from a variety of earlier life forms going back to the early days of our planet.

In thinking about your ancestors, in theory $(2^{81} - 2)$ people were needed in your creation over the last 80 generations or 2,000 years, assuming 25 years between generations. That's a big, big number! (It is much, much larger than your actual number of *unique* ancestors, (still measured in billions), meaning that some relatives were involved more than once in the causal chain of your creation). If we were to draw our unique ancestral tree vertically upwards, it would appear as an inverted pyramid initially, but, if we originated from just a few humans the shape of our ancestral tree would have to change to a diamond. It may be more logical to view life as an inverted "V" shape with all life forms interrelated, arising and dying to further life forms every moment.

If you were to repeat the going back in time experiment at 1,000 years per second, you would eventually see the formation of Planet Earth after 7 to 8 weeks, (4.5 billion years ago), and the "Big Bang" and formation of our universe after a *further* 3.5 months, (13.8 billion years ago). Some scientists theorize that our universe prior to the Big Bang was no larger than a garden pea; and furthermore, that if all the space was taken out of atomic particles, the whole of the human race would fit into the volume of a sugar cube. Based on science like this, can you believe that we are all connected to the same Source? And, moreover, that we are an *integral* and *everlasting* part of that Source given that energy can neither be created nor destroyed only transformed? And, the really amazing thing is the very existence of our universe and its beginnings in the first place with its incredulous amount of *intimately related* energy and matter, (related by Einstein's beautifully simple $e = mc^2$ where e = energy, m = mass of matter and c = the speed of light). The existence of this energy, this universe, is utterly incomprehensible to the intelligence available to human beings. We are the created, not the Creator, albeit co-creating over our human life-span.

The above is a part-summary of what could be a long discourse, indeed a book in its own right, about the origins of life and our universe. Never the less, we boldly suggest that **we are all from the same *Source*, and that furthermore, all life forms including human beings were *formed* from the invisible, indestructible, eternal, *formless energy* that forms all of creation.**

The Oneness Map overleaf, illustrates causal links between Source and each of us, and to keep things simple only the Big Bang and Planet Earth are shown amongst the many planetary forms of our solar system and beyond.

The Oneness Map: your Connection to All-that-Is

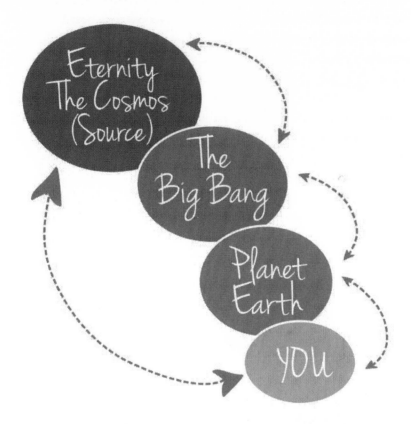

If scientists are correct in believing that our planet derived from a single Big Bang estimated at 13.8 billion years ago, and assuming that this Big Bang itself arose out of the Cosmos or Source or Eternity, then we are all connected to Source by the law of cause and effect – we are intimately connected to everything that preceded us right back to any beginning.

If we are all connected to that original Source, it would make sense that everything is **inter-being** or inter-related with everything else – *and it is,* as can be demonstrated by simply reflecting on ***anything***, such as this paper in front of your eyes if you're reading this book in paper form.

The whole world is in a piece of paper. Paper comes from trees that require the sun, air, earth and water – the elements - in order to exist. The trees were cut down by human beings and processed in a factory requiring people and many additional resources. Everything is inter-related, inter-being or inter-existing with everything else.

All this means that you are forever-Being, (not *a* forever-Being but part of the Oneness), currently expressing life through your human form which is influenced by ego-identity. The difference between you and your corpse, is the life force that reunites, or merges, or simply remains with, the all-pervading consciousness upon your human "death." See Chapter 1 where we discuss logical options for what happens at death. Below and overleaf we tabulate some assumptions underpinning the above discussion and the contents of this book:

---

1. The difference between you and your corpse is your spiritual, formless Being, part of Universal Mind or Big Mind:

Evidence: we appear to weigh the same dead or alive (except for small accountable physical changes); energy can only be transformed not destroyed. Your corpse will show no sign of life, since your spirit/ life force/ Being will remain a part of the One formless realm of Being/ "God"/ All-That-Is.

Implications: start operating as forever-Being immediately, now!! This book will show you how.

---

2. Little mind or ego is partly associated with our physical brain structure:

Evidence: brain damage can affect our thoughts, emotions, feelings, behaviors, memories, motor-skills, etc.

Implications: take good care of your body and mind; operate as forever-Being living in present awareness now

---

3. We have free will:

Evidence: we are free to make choices and decisions as we feel fit and only slowly are more and more people awakening to forever-Being; most people are still trapped in ego rather than observing thoughts impartially, and living in reality

Implications: Until more and more people awaken from their ego-prison there will be continuing insanity and delusional living

---

4. We each come from the One Source that is constantly, infinitely creative every moment:

Evidence: (i) Big Bang originating from singular pea-sized formation; (ii) commonality of elements air, fire, water, earth; (iii) close commonality of human DNA with bananas, rabbits, etc.; (iv) emptiness of the universe and everything in it - the entire human race of some 7 billion people could fit in the volume of a sugar cube if the space between atomic particles was removed; (v) we were each created without any effort on our part; (vi) life is infinitely creating, mushrooming as old forms "die" and new forms "arise" ; (vii) the old and the new are intimately interrelated

Implications (i) We were each created miraculously from billions of ancestors and each of us can trace our essence to the beginning of Planet Earth and our Universe; (ii) we are not separate but all from the same One, (iii) we should have reverence for all life, (iv) we should be at one with the infinite life-flow, not resisting it; (v) we should love everyone (literally) everything – even the furniture in a room is full of aliveness, (vi) entertain the possibility that there is no beginning and no end – yes, that is beyond the human mind; (vii) if we are eternal we'd better get to like it!

5. Our limited human senses misguide complete understanding of reality:

Evidence: Who knows there may be hundreds of different senses in the world and universe – other creatures have different senses (bats, birds, fish etc.); we tend to assume that the interpretations arising from our particular senses is the only way to "see" or sense things. This limits our perception.

Implications: we can only see as our capabilities allow us. What is ultimate reality? We can expand our capacity by seeing as intuitive forever-Being beyond the limited capacities of the ego mind.

6. The aim of *being present* and *aware* as the witness of thoughts and feelings/ emotions is relevant to the well-being of all of us:

Evidence: the choice is between jeopardy and joy – the end of human war, mistreatment and destruction across our planet

Implications: The inner purpose of each of us is to become Present as forever-Being living in reality and sanity this very moment while recognizing our Oneness with Life

7. Operating from forever-Being will be the right path for each of us

Evidence: As forever-Being we can only serve from the infinite flow of light, love and joy, (unimpeded by any sense of me and mine), which must be of benefit to all life that surrounds us

Implications: Operating from forever-Being, your legacy will take care of itself. (In any case, who cares about your legacy 20 or 50 years after you have "died?")

The best any of us can do is to follow our heart and if our ego does take us over and get the better of us sometimes it is a human trait! We just have to recognize and minimize ego-interference; call this ego-management if you will, moment to moment. It is also mind-body management as our mood and state of "Being" are influenced by how physically relaxed we are, where we place our attention, how readily we embrace our emotions and how calm our mind is. And these are affected by such things as exercise, diet, quantity of sleep, daily habits, the way that we handle demands on our time and the environment we choose or find ourselves in.

As we have noted, the difference between you and your corpse is your life force, (animating presence, your Being, consciousness, Big Mind), operating within and without you. This Being is the timeless, formless, forever real you, the permanent spiritual you having a brief human experience, yet interwoven with the one life of the universe.

This "Being" dimension is distinct from the ego dimension. Remember that the ego, (which by the way is to be appreciated and respected, not made into an enemy), is the conditioned self-image built around our temporary and precarious human existence. In its most vulnerable form the ego needs constant validation and approval to make up for its sense of lack, for example, in comparison to others. It can be important for the vulnerable ego to keep up appearances in the eyes of family, friends and other people in our lives, even strangers. This can lead to fear – oh what will they think of me, will they be happy with my choices? While it is necessary to consider people impacted by our choices and behavior, living a full, free and happy life following our heart will benefit the people around us. We have to take care not to *identify* with the human ego, just observe it, and remind ourselves that we cannot possibly be the temporary thoughts that come and go, but the ongoing awareness of those thoughts.

Being and ego can be construed as two dimensions as illustrated in the Human Being Map depicted overleaf, although ultimately they are one, since consciousness is oneness of Source. Note that pure Being and ego cannot co-exist, just as darkness cannot exist in the presence of light.

You have always been *you,* throughout your life as a baby, a small child, pre high school, and teenager, adolescent, adult. Is it not the same unchanging you who is aware of all these changes? Your body cells too have changed so many times, and your current body reflects your current age. The real you is forever-Being. Chop off a limb, lose an eye or replace an internal organ ... and you are still you ... change a thought, emotion or belief ... and you are still you. Die to the human body and you are still you – assuming you haven't experienced your own death before, you may have to take that one on faith. Again we come to the notion that there is a difference between you and your corpse which is the life force itself. Your awareness has been constant and unchanging throughout. So wake up! Realize that you *are* the awareness – the awareness that sees/ senses the external world *and* the internal world of temporary thoughts and emotions that come and go. Identification with these thoughts and emotions, especially painful ones is the main cause of psychological suffering and bondage of human beings.

THE HUMAN BEING MAP: DIMENSIONS OF EGO AND FOREVER-BEING

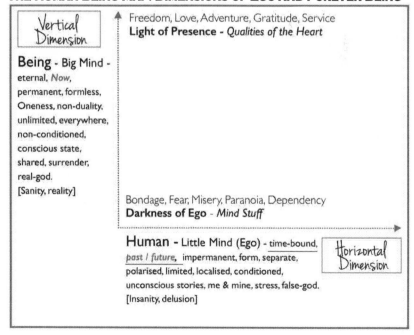

How should we view such thoughts and emotions?

1. Realize that you are not your thoughts and emotions that *come and go*, albeit they may be related to your experiences, conditioned thought-emotion patterns and current life situation.

2. Observe your thoughts and emotions and try to put to space around them. Ask yourself questions like "where is the thinker?", "who is the thinker?", "where did that thought come from?" and "what is my next thought going to be?"

3. Realize that thoughts of a troubling kind are often untrue, perhaps biased by earlier conditioning, and don't take them so seriously. But do list genuine concerns for attention in writing to get them off of your mind.

4. Quiet or stop your thinking by *directing attention away from your mind*, for example, by using a simple meditation/ breathing technique and/or focusing attention on the body, thereby withdrawing attention from mind activity. A regular "body scan" can help, involving just observation, (or including deliberate relaxation), of the whole body or just chosen parts such as the hands.

5. Realize that in the absence of the ego mind, there is a gap of "No-Mind" that opens you up to the "Clarity of Big Mind", a deeper sensory perception. (Refer to the No Mind Map overleaf).

Your *natural* state is one of being relaxed and joyful. If you suffer this is generally through identification with, being lost in, the trance of involuntary automatic thought. And, associated therewith, it is not the seemingly unfortunate events that make us suffer, rather the meaning we attribute to events. This is not to deny that events such as the loss of a loved one, for example, have the capacity to shake us up. Yet with the right mind-set that really understands the nature of life, and monitoring and evaluating the stories running through our minds, we can cope much better than otherwise.

When operating from ego, your *Sense of Self* comes from the *stuff* (or content) in one's mind. When operating from (forever) Being, your Sense of Self comes from Presence, now – the natural flow of Joy, Love Light and Gratitude free of mental commentary and sufferings of your ego lost in stories of past or future.

THE NO MIND MAP—MEDITATION AND MINDFULNESS

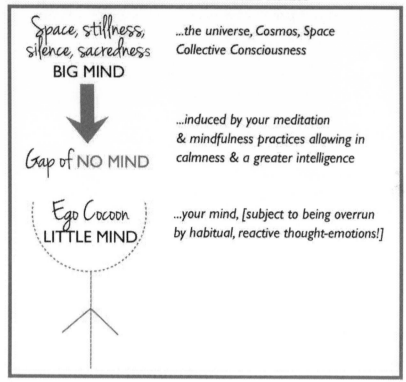

Space, stillness, silence, sacredness
BIG MIND

...the universe, Cosmos, Space
Collective Consciousness

Gap of NO MIND

...induced by your meditation
& mindfulness practices allowing in
calmness & a greater intelligence

Ego Cocoon
LITTLE MIND

...your mind, [subject to being overrun
by habitual, reactive thought-emotions!]

Here are a few helpful techniques:

1. Byron Katie's "The Work" for questioning the validity of thoughts and beliefs, and bringing in more joy

2, Eckhart Tolle's suggestion of anchoring presence in the body – essentially diverting attention energy from our mind to our body, quieting the former

3. Sedona method for letting go of difficult emotions

4. If you are calm, or can get calm, simply stop thinking if you can, but don't suppress thoughts/ emotions, observe them impartially, without judgment; and thereby de-energize them

5. Routinely check that your body is relaxed and that your mind is calm. Focus on following your breath, in and out, saying to yourself words like calm, clear, beyond

6. Ask yourself questions like:

(a) Am I calm and relaxed now?

(b) Am I feeling good now?

(c) Am I smelling the roses now? (I.e. am I present? And, a reminder to focus on your breath)

(d) What problem do I have right now? [Generally the answer is "none," albeit you may have made a list and a schedule to deal with some matters of importance from a state of calm presence].

(e) Am I the "Body" or the "Animating Presence?"

7. Surrender and accept "what-is" without resistance – if nothing fazes you, you are strong not weak

8. You have experienced difficult times and worried needlessly – remember that they never lasted. Remind yourself "This too shall pass." And ask yourself "what am I afraid of losing?" But, do not ruminate. Get into the "State of Presence."

9. Whatever has happened, have you noticed that throughout your whole life you're still here? The ongoing observing awareness.

10. Say to yourself, 'I don't mind what happens" in life since first, it has happened anyway so you can't change that, and secondly, you have decided that it will not disturb your peace of mind and you will deal with it, if action or change is warranted, from a calm place.

We are not suggesting that recognizing your forever-Being, and surrendering to real life, means being passive. On the contrary, life is to be faced fully and turned into a joyous adventure, learning along the way from missteps, mistakes and misfortunes. When challenges arise, slow down, stay calm and deal with them boldly from your Being, your access to Big Mind. You're still here, haven't gone anywhere or changed *in your deep essence*, have you?

As forever-Being, living in reality and sanity, there is nothing for you to fear other than the self-imposed barriers and excuses of the false ego. Manage the ego well, and relax!! And, remember that as forever-Being you live life in the vertical dimension, this timeless moment, now.

Why are you here?

Making the most of being here on Planet Earth is the main theme of this book. The short answer to the question of *"why are you here?"* is to express life – the life that flows through you as a result of being alive. We could say that you are here to express your unique talents and calling – and that would be right – although it may take some trial and error before you feel to be on the right track. And, when that happens, you may be able to look back and "connect the dots" that led you to your purpose. Your talents can be developed through your natural abilities, heart-felt interests and application and in response to your experiences and life situation.

You're here to be you, "everyone else has been taken," as Oscar Wilde pointed out.

Your presence here on planet Earth can be traced back to the beginning of time, (if there was a beginning), as discussed above. You are an integral and unique part of *all that is*. Life is expressing itself through you, and given a free will through deliberate use of your thoughts and feelings, you are now expressing yourself over your short human-life span. We may consider that we are each but a speck of human existence – even a "very good innings," a life span of say 100 years is *infinitesimal* compared to the life of Planet Earth or the Universe or even to the period of evolution of human life forms.

We can infer from this, that:
(a) We are relatively insignificant!
(b) We are very special and unique!

Note though that (a) applies to our very temporary form, not our eternal, permanent essence and Oneness while (b) is associated with our brief sojourn, this present golden opportunity, as a temporary form on Planet Earth.

It should make us all wonder what's really important in our lives and wonder whether things we regard as so important are really that important at all!

When we learn about the tragic lives of some people – for example alcoholics who die at 40 or so from cirrhosis of the liver – we may wonder why they wasted their time lost in a sad spiral of negative thoughts, emotions and behaviors, not knowing that they had the choice of a glorious, even joyful life. We might consider that they drowned in their ego recognizing that their pain came from identifying with negative thoughts and emotions. If people only knew that it is unnecessary to cling to these unwanted thoughts and feelings, the world would be a far happier place. The sooner that humanity moves out of ego, (thought identification, little mind), and into forever-Being (awareness, big mind) the better!

Realize deeply too, that you are at the *very forefront* of all creation with a long trail of "death and life," (which is just continuous, ongoing transformation), behind you. Right now, billions of years have passed in the Cosmos, and none of the future has yet arrived.

And, we, life, are continually evolving as the crest of life moves, advances, ever forward. We can hardly imagine what humans might evolve too, what new brain elements may appear as we hope for peace on Earth and the elimination of suffering.

According to the Buddha, there is no reason not to live in a continuous *State of Love, Joy and Gratitude.* Eckhart Tolle suggests that we need always to live in *acceptance, enjoyment or enthusiasm* in whatever we do. Aristotle also directed our attention to enjoyment and enthusiasm. The fact is that we do have a choice and that may mean dropping your reasons and your stories. Why you say, how? Yes I say, just drop them and pay *attention* to the good stuff! It *really is* your choice. This doesn't mean that life is always a pleasant "bowl of cherries," but remember that it's *the way we see things* that makes a situation feel bad, good or indifferent. Get into the habit of seeing the opportunity in any apparent misfortune, and, before judging ego-driven behavior in others, look at your own reactions. And, further, remember that as forever-Being, you are the witness of thoughts – not the thoughts themselves. Above all, master your choice of where to focus your attention.

Ultimately, each of us is here to bring presence, (and hence reality and sanity), into the world. In this regard, you are only as aware, present or enlightened now as you can be this very moment. Your presence is only now, and not a goal for the future; yet your daily commitment to operating as forever-Being, being physically relaxed, surrendered to what-is, and maintaining a calm, clear mind – using ways appropriate to you to maintain this State – will help you to be more present, this very moment now. To stop thinking when you want to, or at least to calm the observed mind through *deliberate shifts in attention*, is synonymous both with being present now and living as forever- Being.

In cessation of, or non-identification with thinking, we open up to the wider intelligence of Big Mind. We still need to think conventionally – but hopefully not at 4am when we actually need sleep! If you do get caught out by some worry at 4am, perhaps, for example, you feel the need to respond to something important, keep a bedside notepad and schedule a time at a more reasonable hour to deal with the matter; then withdraw attention from the mind, (to your breath or inner-body energy field for example), so that you can sleep well. A systematic relaxation of the body from head to toe may be very helpful. You may find that noticing your breath and deliberately extending the length of your out-breath will get you off to sleep. In the worst case scenario, should you find that you're unable to stop thinking, try at least to feel gratitude for your many blessings, the good in your life. Take solace that you're safe and that there's no man (or woman) eating tiger in the room!

In essence, we each need to move from the prison of our "me and mine" ego cocoon to what the Buddha called emptiness, or what Jesus called the fullness of life. Emptiness refers to clearing our minds, and freedom from unhelpful conditioning and paradigms, while fullness of life refers to unblocking ourselves, (same as emptiness), and allowing the creative life energy to work through us. Moreover, we can deliberately assist the process by changing our objects of attention and choice of environments, thereby uncovering our true nature more in alignment with the divine.

PART 1: Manifesting Destiny

CHAPTER 1

The RAFTS Map: Results-Actions-Feelings-Thoughts-State

A

s we will see in due course, the RAFTS Map: "Results-Actions-Feelings-Thoughts-State" depicted overleaf can be presented and explained in different ways. The causal relationship between thoughts, feelings, actions and results is already well recognized. Connecting one's State (of Consciousness) to this cause and effect logic is a vitally important addition, because it enables a shift to seeing through the *eyes of Being* rather than the ego, a dramatic and life changing shift in perspective.

The RAFTS Map founded on our *State of Consciousness* will help us to ensure that our manifestations in life are congruent with who we are, and therefore fulfilling. It will help ensure that our ladder of purpose is up against the right wall, so that we don't waste time or energy achieving and manifesting things which turn out to be of not that much value to us or others. Connected thereto, we want our manifestations to be effective, efficient, fulfilling and purposeful so that we live more happily, and make the best use of our short time on Planet Earth.

In the RAFTS Map shown overleaf, there is a causal relationship between observable actions and results. This is why it is so important to take action in order to manifest our goals, and not to rely solely on the "thoughts become things" axiom. Indeed, it is the underlying feelings, e-motions and thoughts that provoke or motivate our actions. Never the less, as we take action, we may well find that the Universe seems to be supporting us with helpful coincidences and synchronicities beyond our own direct actions. This may be evident in the present or may be in retrospect as we review life events. Could it be that our thoughts, which are energy forms, impact wider collective consciousness? Many believe this to be so, consider, for example, Jung's "collective unconsciousness." We make no claims and you will have to evaluate according to your own life experiences.

THE RAFTS MAP — MANIFESTING RESULTS

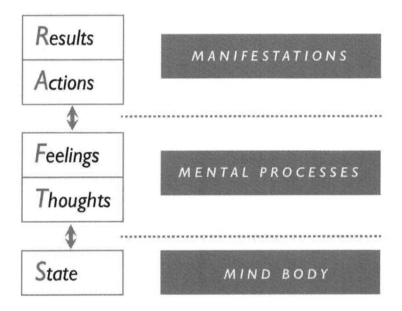

The Map suggests a causal relationship between (the quality of) our feelings and thoughts and our underlying State which includes our overall mood, and whether we tend to operate from a relatively closed ego-perspective within the limitations of our experientially conditioned, "ego-cocoon," or from a more open and aware one. Let's look in more detail now at each element of the Map.

State

We look at this aspect of the Map in more detail first since it is the foundation. You may have come across the expression "we see things as we are" attributed to Anais Nin among others. This is our "State," the way we see things, which is a function of our mood and our state of Being-ness versus operating out of ego.

Our mind-body state concerns where we are coming from and what we give out to the world, what's in us, and how we show up. That is why, in the Introduction to this book we considered the notions of forever-Being and our Oneness with all life going backwards in time and into the future. The concept of oneness also fits in perfectly with the Buddha's notion of non-self.

In simplistic terms, at any given moment we feel good or we feel bad. The state that we feel to be in at any moment can depend upon many mind-body factors, including our genetic disposition, habits (sleep, diet, exercise, physiology, work, recreation, etc.), the environment, the conditioning and lifestyle that we experience, the extent to which our needs for well-being are met, as well as the interplay between thoughts and emotions that we allow ourselves to be engaged in. The good news is that we have a measure of control over all of these with the possible exception of genetic disposition, although relatively new research in epigenetics suggests that this can be modified too! (Dispenza et al).

THE ABCD MAP — MOODS RELATED TO FOREVER-BEING, EGO

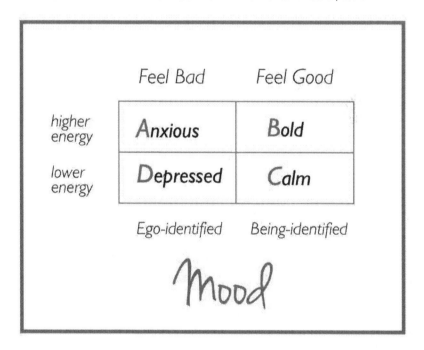

With reference to the "ABCD Map" above, essentially if we are to attract good fulfilling things into our lives, we need to be in a *feel good*, abundant and grateful mode which is consistent with the State of Being as opposed to the State of

Ego or identification with lack, not enough, "more, more, more" and associated therewith "I'll be happy when ..... ." (Fill in the blank).

The ABCD Map suggests that we should take steps to ensure that our mood be both calm and bold, and thereby avoid anxiety and depression. It is important to check that your body is relaxed, and it is helpful to maintain consciousness of your inner body energy. With the right mind-set, there is no need for anxiety or fear in the present moment, and particularly in a safe and comfortable environment. Meditation is helpful to becoming calm and present; it can also help you to be bold or fearless, through stopping and looking deeply at the true nature of reality and transformation of life forms.

With reference to the "Awareness/ Consciousness Map" below, if there is any guarantee of happiness and fulfillment in life, then being in touch with the Oneness of creation, our Creator is that guarantee.

THE AWARENESS/ CONSCIOUSNESS MAP

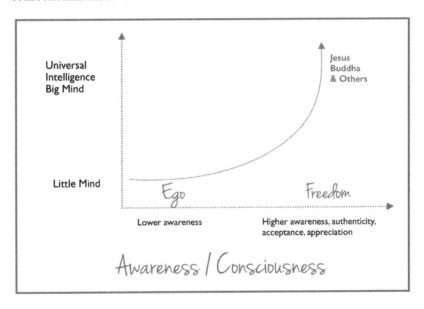

The first commandment of Jesus is to love God, (or your Source or Creator), with all your heart, all your soul and all your mind. The Buddha recognized the Oneness of reality through the notion of inter-Being and interconnectedness of the elements of sun, water, air and earth as discussed in the "Introduction."

Buddhists refer to the "Ultimate Dimension" which is likened to the Ocean, (and similar to the "vertical dimension" shown on the Human Being Map provided in the Introduction). The waves that come and go are always in touch with the mighty Ocean. Similarly we can think of humans, (like waves), as being in touch with their Creator or Being or God, (like the Ocean). The Buddha reminded us of the impermanence of all forms, of the beauty of silence and stillness, and opened our eyes to peace, love, joy, acceptance, gratitude and interconnectedness in the present moment.

Jesus and Buddha were aware people in touch with reality, (not the oft-times inaccurate, automatic, fleeting thoughts that pass for reality), with qualities that included awareness, authenticity, acceptance and appreciation – explored in Chapter 2, the AAAA Map.

Now, we are not getting into religion here, only the wisdom of highly notable historical figures. Similar wisdom is found across the various faiths. In their own ways, both Buddha and Jesus taught us (a) how to live (and love) well, (b) how to manage our ego and (c) how to be more present in the here and now. If we could see and sense the world through the eyes of the enlightened Buddha or Jesus and other luminaries we would get as close as possible to the aware state of forever-Being as opposed to the state of ego.

So, what would your perspectives and views on the world be, if you could live in a state of awareness, and see through the eyes of forever-Being? Well, they would undoubtedly transform your life for the better, no matter how happy and successful you are already. With reference to the table overleaf, there are marked differences between seeing through the Eyes of forever-Being rather than the Eyes of Ego.

STATE OF AWARENESS AND PERSPECTIVE ON THE WORLD: EYES OF FOREVER-BEING VERSUS EYES OF EGO

Eyes of Ego [fear]	Eyes of forever-Being [love]
Ego-identified, Impermanent	Forever-Being, awareness
Needy, lacking	Complete, enough
Living in the limited ego's "Comfort Zone"	Living in the amazing Divine's "Comfort Zone!"
Unaware of body's energy	In touch with your life-energy
Mood tied to externals	Joy within, no matter what!
Judgmental	Accept what-is, love what-is
Attachment to me and mine; I'll be happy when …	Detachment from ego-needs; Happy now and always!
Resistance to life	Surrendered; let go, let God
Trapped in past and future	Present moment focus
Exaggerated sense of self (e.g. I am this body)	Realization of Awareness (e.g. I am the animating presence)
Victim of circumstance	Master of destiny
Dissatisfied	Fulfilled
Drama – always something!!	Peace!
Unconscious; self-sabotage	Conscious, wise choices
Identification with involuntary self-talk, my stories	Co-creator; if it's to be it's up to me; conscious focus on mission
Striving, struggle	Inspired action
Resentment, unforgiving	Forgiving (or nothing to forgive)
Anger, dislike	Love and compassion
Limiting beliefs	I can do it; an inner knowing
"Monkey mind," living in illusion	Clarity, living in reality as it is
Anxious	Calm and Bold
Unconscious trance, possessed by mind	Conscious, don't mind what happens
Burdened by worries	Seldom if ever worried
The Good Old days!	Now is perfect!
Life is a battle!	Life is a breeze!

Imagine a conversation with a tree.

QUESTION TO THE TREE	THE TREE'S ANSWER
What's the time?	I don't understand. It's now, it's always now
Oh, you're so much bigger than that tree over there. You must be very proud?	So what! That's just the way I was made. It's the same for all the trees be they bigger, or smaller, less leaves, more leaves, etc. They were made that way by our awesome Creator; all are perfect and as intended according to seed and environmental conditions

Of course, there are major differences between us and trees. In particular, we are able to move around and have highly developed thought and feeling processes. Yet, the conversation with the tree exemplifies that in nature, everything (including you), is already enough and it couldn't be otherwise. All life forms manifest according to earlier life forms and environmental conditions. You are perfect, even perfectly imperfect, as is everyone else. It's just the wonderful way that you were made.

In seeing through the eyes of forever-Being, your temporary automatic, repetitive style of thoughts and feelings would take a lowly second place to your permanent field of awareness. [Recall in the "Introduction" that we explained awareness simply as that constant field of awareness of your life that has always been with you, as your body and mind has changed considerably up to the present day]. Seeing through the eyes of forever-Being, you would not automatically get lost in and follow all thoughts and urges as if they were commands, rather you would view them in a non-judgmental manner and consider their veracity. You are *not* your thoughts.

As you go through life, it is fundamentally important to *maintain a relaxed state at all times,* to *maintain zero resistance to life,* and to take timely action if appropriate according to situations arising. Relaxation is common to meditation, visualization, hypnosis and mind-management techniques such as neuro-linguistic programming (NLP) and the "Silva Method."

Now, imagine that:

(1) You *are* the present moment – free of the burdens of time and

thoughts

Try it now. How does it feel like to actually *be* the present moment? Can you sense the stillness, spaciousness? Look! Listen! Stop and observe your breath without trying to control it. On the in breath say inwardly *I Am* and on the out-breath say *the Now*. Don't just say it – slow down, be still, and sense it, feel it. You will find your real self by coming into the present. If there are any lingering thoughts and emotions just observe them and they should settle down, dissolve. There are no problems now as you read this. Even if under physical attack you would be far too busy dealing with the situation rather than spending time to worry about it.

(2) You *are* one with life – free of separation, on the wave of the life

continuum

You are not your temporary life situation, you are life itself. You were created by your Creator and your life can be traced all the way back through your ancestors, to the Big Bang, and beyond. And, this moment, alive, you are at the very forefront of creation, among the freshest and latest life forms having a human experience.

The real you, your life force never dies. You may want to think of this real you as part of the divine, the eternal or permanent. Feel the aliveness, your life-energy in your body, *as often as you can*, (which also diverts attention from the mind). Let this be your anchor in the present, peace *from* mind. [You may prefer other anchors such as your breath or invent one such as your halo].

(3) You are here in the *temporary human form* for the sole purpose of en-**joy**ing yourself in alignment with the direction, aliveness and joy of

your Maker, contributing your gifts to the world

Decide to live from the joy of your Creator, that is, to live from love – a warm reverence and appreciation for the sacredness of life – rather than from fear. And, you will do this *whatever happens!* This could be the most important choice of your life, more important than your choice of partner, career or home. For-

get any excuses that your mind comes up with and find a way. And, if you worry about being selfish, take it to heart that if you are a joy, it's guaranteed that
you will be a joy to others.

According to Ralph Waldo Emerson "We lie in the lap of immense intelligence,
which makes us receivers of its truth and organs of its activity. When we discern justice, when we discern truth, we do nothing of ourselves, but allow a
passage to its beams."

The above quotation is consistent with Jesus' remark that "it is the father who
doeth the works," and his advice to "deny thyself."

These quotes can be considered as cues from excellent sources to allow divinity
to guide us, and perhaps not to take ourselves too seriously. Since we were created through a higher power and didn't create ourselves "let go, let God."

Accordingly, we should neither push ourselves so hard that we frazzle ourselves
and others in the process, nor beat ourselves up when things turn out a bit
awry. So long as we have good intentions and are willing to learn we can live in
a calm, relaxed and accepting manner.

You will surely experience adversities. These will develop your strength of
character, so, with this understanding, learn to accept if not enjoy the process!

Know that birth and death are simply life transitions that are absolutely necessary for life itself. When your time is up, it's time for renewal that's all. Life *is*
change, and without change and renewal there would be no life. As the saying
goes "the only *constant* is change." Fear not! Be bold!!

With reference to the "Create your World Map" overleaf, you create your
world through your awareness, self-mastery and what you give out to the
world. As you give so you will receive. As within, so without.

THE CREATE YOUR WORLD MAP – GIVING AND GETTING

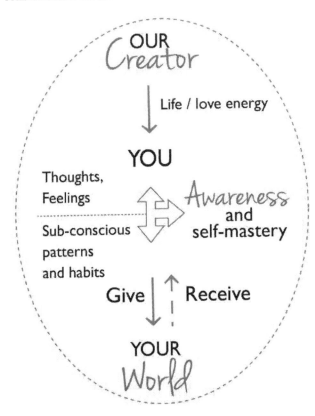

In the state of awareness you are the watcher of your thoughts. In awareness you observe your thoughts, feelings, beliefs and stories non-judgmentally and choose where to place your attention. Developing self-mastery, you have the power to choose or change the content of your thoughts, especially to maintain positive ones always. Through consistent, daily affirmation and imagination, you can impress upon your sub-conscious beneficial changes in how you see and feel about life, and manifest your desires. Deliberate and conscious repetition will rewire your brain and result in forming, (a few, very specific), good habits that support your growth. [Refer Chapter 12].

If you can ensure that you are present, in a very relaxed state, your brain waves will be at alpha or theta so that the intensity and rate of thought generation is subdued. At the same time your powers of creative imagination and intuition will increase. In aware, *appreciative presence*, there is no negativity or anxiety and no problems. And, this is not a numbed state but a highly alert one.

You can achieve the state of calm awareness, that sees interconnected reality clearly and freshly in the here and now, untainted by harmful thoughts.

You are 100% safe – free of fear.

The Creator gives you love. Your ego gives you fear. You seek no salvation or release in the future, and all that you could possibly ever need is met already, secure in the knowledge that all to come will be good too. Welcome everything.

Operating from the state of awareness, you are relaxed and calm, surrendered to, (not resisting), what-is. In your essence you are already whole and complete while your body and thoughts-emotions are temporary or impermanent to use a Buddhist expression. It's easy to recognize that your thoughts and emotions are fleeting and temporary; in cosmic terms your body is equally as fleeting. Just compare, for example, a typical life span of say 80 years with the age of this planet 4.5 billion years. Yet life goes on, always will, always has, and your so-called birth and death are merely transitions in the life continuum.

You can think of your awareness as the forever-Being side of you, and your thoughts, feelings and senses as the human side of you. Similarly, with reference to Jesus Christ, you can choose to associate "Christ," (the Messiah, the anointed one), with the forever-Being or divine side of Jesus Christ, and to think of "Jesus" as the human side.

In stark contrast to the commonplace, ego-driven up and down mood-states experienced in reaction to, or with, the external world, living from awareness or state of forever-Being frees us from ego-driven mind chatter, (the "monkey mind" as it is sometimes called). This enables us to experience an inner peace and calm. Indeed, in order to be in touch with our Creator, we have to drop our ego and sense of self. We have to get out of our own way, and a key ingredient of that is to be present in the here and now, rather than lost in compulsive thought of the ego. You are eternal awareness, not the fleeting and temporary thoughts and emotions!

Thoughts and Feelings

The interplay between thoughts and feelings is of fundamental importance, since on the one hand they influence our State, and on the other, govern our actions, (expressed as behavior), and our results. There is a need to differentiate between automatic, involuntary thoughts on the one hand, and conscious, that is to say deliberate thought, on the other. When following automatic, repetitive thoughts, you are lost in trance, possessed by thought and associated emotions - you could say that your mind is using you. In deliberate thought mode, you are the master of your thoughts and you are using them productively.

Indeed, the human condition is such that many of our thoughts are repetitive, automatic, involuntary, patterned and habitual, that is to say conditioned over many years, especially during childhood when our mind-set and beliefs were being shaped and formed. Buddhists believe that this conditioning goes back further to our ancestors, and that karma can impact our future lives.

Gaining conscious and deliberate control of our thoughts and feelings is crucial for anyone who wishes to live life on their own terms, and to live life by purposeful design rather than simply conforming to the cultural conditioning of society.

A few things to note about our thoughts and emotions: first, our thoughts are creating 24/7!! Our brains are unbelievably active energetically in processing sensory information and this includes thoughts – typically 60,000 each day according to some scientists. Although thoughts are fleeting and impermanent, "thought-trains" can draw us in if we are not alert and take us over – don't let that happen to you unless they're pleasant ones! "This too will pass" – be it good or bad.

Secondly, thoughts are only a minor aspect of intelligence; for example, your body has much greater intelligence than your mind given the mind-boggling feats it produces in keeping you alive and healthy every second – it just happens; and, for those who believe in consciousness pervading everything animate or otherwise, an individual's thoughts and emotions are infinitely microscopic entities of energy compared to the awesome, inconceivably vast energy of the universe.

Thirdly, the quality of our thoughts, emotions (and state) will vastly improve if we learn to live in a calm, relaxed manner in the here and now. Being present now implies acceptance of what is, and is true freedom because we are not wrapped up in the past or future. Yet being present is an excellent state to consciously engage our quietened thoughts and emotions in planning, direction setting, establishing goals and milestones, and engaging with our vision of the future.

All this means that we should take care not to be identified with, and get possessed by, negative feel bad thoughts and emotions of little mind or ego, that cause us to act unconsciously and unwisely. On the contrary, we can actively monitor our thoughts and substitute positive ones for negative ones. We should be still, calm and present in the here and now in order to be in touch with, and guided by, the creative universal intelligence that is behind, precedes, and drives, all life.

If a thought that doesn't serve you passes over your field of awareness, you can ignore it, perhaps substituting an opposite positive thought. Important thoughts arising about actions you may need to take can be listed so that you can get them off of your mind as noted earlier. In some cases, immediate action may be beneficial but beware of following thoughts blindly, which is indulging in unconsciousness.

This will become a mind-habit. "You will be transformed by the renewing of your mind" to paraphrase Romans 2:12 of the Bible. In Corinthians 10.5 of the Bible there is a reference to "bringing every thought into captivity to the obedience of Christ …" This suggests that we need to discipline our thoughts. Furthermore, "A man reaps what he sows," as stated in Galatians 6.7, which leads us into the next section on action and results.

Action and Results

What do you really want? With the caveat, beware what you wish for! Goals, the results we seek as human beings, can come from either the human (ego) part of us, or from the forever-Being (higher awareness/ consciousness) part of us.

Ego driven goals are more concerned with protecting our vulnerable ego, for example the need to prove oneself, or look good, or gain approval, or meet some other sense of lack – all perhaps quite normal given the plight of the typical human being, growing up and adapting to society's norms, expectations and pressures!

Achievement of ego driven goals may satisfy us for a while, and may even be necessary, to end an unsatisfactory situation such as negative net worth, or to teach us a lesson. In our early working years we will be concerned to ensure that we have a roof over our heads and sufficient funds to take care of ourselves and our dependents. But ultimately, the never-ending quest for "more, more, more" beyond important needs is not fulfilling of itself, as it suggests that we are never really satisfied except perhaps for brief intervals when certain goals have been accomplished. On the question of work or retirement, we need to be contributing and providing service in one way or another to channel our life energies and this is covered in later chapters. The important thing is that we maintain a healthy state of wellbeing, and are guided by love rather than driven by fear as in "keeping up with the Joneses," approval-seeking, excessive neediness or blindly following societies dictates.

Higher awareness goals are more concerned with our feeling of oneness with the source or life force that permeates our world and beyond; operating boldly when appropriate from a calm, clear, fresh and undistracted mind in the present moment. And, in a feel good state of presence we can set goals from a deeper and more fulfilling inspirational level, guided by higher awareness and wisdom. Good or great results come from a growth mind-set based on a clear purpose, and engage our strengths, values and preferences. Yet, do not be attached to your goals, their achievement is secondary to your participation in the game of life.

When operating from forever-Being rather than ego, your goals will be stress-free, and you will feel a sense of passion or love-energy. It isn't really so important whether you gain or lose, fail or succeed every time, living from forever-Being you will grow.

With respect to ambition, there's nothing wrong in wanting to contribute more in life, be that through a more influential job position or through an expanding business in which you have an ownership stake and are able to provide job opportunities that contribute to society. In a sense, there is nothing inherently wrong with any choice; it's just that wiser choices connected to forever-Being are likely to make you and others around you happier. As you sow, you shall reap and the law of attraction is invoked.

If you have a driving force to acquire, so long as you have a clear purpose, are being true to your values, and you are experiencing real joy and fulfillment, particularly in your relationships, then that's fine too. There is no guilt living from spirit or forever-Being! In determining your way ahead, consider suggestions for "moving toward lasting happiness" provided by Chopra and Tanzi in their book "Super Brain – Unleash the Explosive Power of your Mind."

- Give of yourself. Take care of others, and care for them.
- Work at something you love
- Set worthy long-range goals that will take years to achieve
- Be open minded
- Have emotional resilience
- Learn from the past, and then put it behind you. Live for the present
- Plan for the future without anxiety, fear or dread
- Develop close, warm social bonds

Chopra and Tanzi also advise on not what to do. Don't:

- Hitch your happiness to external rewards
- Postpone being happy until sometime in the future
- Expect someone else to make you happy
- Equate happiness with momentary pleasure
- Pursue more and more stimulation
- Allow your emotions to become habitual and stuck
- Close yourself off from new experiences
- Ignore the signals of inner tension and conflict
- Dwell on the past or live in fear of the future

These lists fit in well with the main themes presented in this book, and the premise that attending to your own wellbeing and inner strength is a prerequisite to a full, adventurous life.

Feeling is the Secret

In the RAFTS Map we know that *feelings* lead directly into action. When we feel inspired, we experience *inspired action,* which is the ideal because then we feel *enthusiasm.* The next best feeling to have is enjoyment, and below that, at least acceptance. In mindfulness is the intention to enjoy and appreciate everything, even what we often tend to regard as household chores such as washing the dishes. We can achieve this by deciding to focus close attention on the doing of the thing before us, and not to spend this time in unproductive thinking.

In reality, feeling is not a separate phenomenon but interplays with thoughts or imaginations, perceptions, interpretations, questions, ideas, etc. that come to us. In the law of attraction we get what we focus on, what we give our attention to. We also need to have a vibrational match or feeling for that which we desire, and if we affirm or imagine something, it must feel true to us. On the other hand, doing things now, whether we feel like it or not, is a master skill, (although in some cases we may indeed need to wait until we are in the right frame of mind, so long as we do not indulge in unnecessary excessive procrastination).

There was a book published way-back in 1944 by a popular author named Neville Goddard, (who wrote simply under the name "Neville"), called *Feeling is the Secret.* The main emphasis in that book was on adopting "the feeling of the wish fulfilled" in order to manifest goals. In other words, Neville suggested using our imagination to feel the presence of what we desire *as if* it was *already* manifest. This invites us to engage in mental movies, using our imagination to "preview life's coming attractions" as Einstein put it.

In support of this from the scientific community, experiments have been carried out with athletes where their performance (manifestations) of sports related goals has improved by *imagining* or visualizing their physical actions and "being there," fully associated with the mental movie. This is linked to the scientifically verified fact that our minds cannot tell the difference between a real and imagined event.

This is why vivid dreams seem real to us and our body physiology and so on can react as if our dreams and imaginings were real. Correspondingly, neuroscientists have found that imagination of phenomena and their actual reality cause similar brain activity.

Below we show a different representation of the RAFTS Map, with *feeling* as the central aspect in manifesting results. This Map is consistent with our experience that our feelings are affected not only by our thoughts but by our state of awareness, (or mood and Being-ness), our actions, and our results or manifestations.

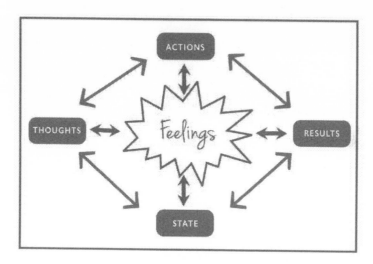

Indeed, we are feeling beings, and consciously or otherwise, we tend to gravitate towards things that give us pleasure, and move away from things that give us pain. We also live in accordance with our values and needs which will include a concern for others to a higher or lesser degree. It is generally recognized that where there is a difference between our thoughts and emotions, that our emotion is a more true reflection of how things are, the way we see things.

While thoughts lead to feelings, it can happen the other way round too. Your body, for example, may sense a chemical imbalance which you sense as a feeling, causing you to think I want a cup of caffeinated coffee or a sugary chocolate bar.

Consulting our feelings is something that we need to do on a regular basis, to consider how we feel about our current life situation, and to make choices and decisions about the future.

And, excitingly, we can learn to manage our feelings positively through gratitude and kindness, through our physiology, through exercise, through attention to our inner state, (for example, using meditation), through choice of environment, and through our diet and sleep routines. Managing our mood is covered in more detail in Chapter 7.

In a controversial book written by the late David Hawkins, called Power versus Force, "power" equates to what we refer to as *feel good,* and force equates to what we refer to as *feel bad.* Any positive feeling from courage upwards is termed "power" by Hawkins, while any negative feeling below courage is termed "force."

In the power mode we feel strong, while in the force mode we feel weak. Hawkins attempted to measure the strength of this feeling in human subjects, using, what he called the *muscle test,* for assessing the "truth" of certain statements given to subjects. He originally used the term "kinesiology" for this approach but changed it after the scientific community rallied against his use of this term.

The controversy really concerned the objectivity of measurements, not the basic thrust of his main work. So, rather than throw the baby out with the bathwater, overleaf we reproduce his Power versus Force scale. So long as we accept that there might be some subjectivity in his measures, then his work provides some valuable insights.

In the Hawkins typology overleaf, feelings and emotions are summarized. Compassion, gratitude, empathy and (happy) surprises are not specifically mentioned for example, but reverence and love are associated with these emotions. Hawkins "Power" is similar to the notion of "Awareness" and "Seeing from forever-Being" used in this book, while "Force" aligns with "Seeing from Ego" or being trapped in ego.

Interestingly, desire is seen as negative and this is because of its association with cravings – I'll be happy when … The issue is whether our desire is driven by love or fear and whether we can accept all of our manifestations without disappointment, knowing that we often need to fail our way to success. If our ancestors had not acted on their desire to improve things we might all have remained cavemen, or still be walking miles to find water, so appropriate desire is helpful.

Indeed, if we are uncomfortable with something affecting us directly, desire or self-love may drive us to make changes to become more comfortable. A sincere love of family may drive us to "improve our lot," and make the lives and prospects for our family rosier, and this desire doesn't have to be ego-driven.

POWER VERSUS FORCE SCALE

Feeling	"Truth" Measure	Emotion	Life View
Enlightenment	600 - 1,000	Ineffable	Is
Peace	600	Bliss	Perfect
Joy	540	Serenity	Complete
Love	500	Reverence	Benign
Reason	400	Understanding	Meaningful
Acceptance	350	Forgiveness	Harmonious
Willingness	300	Optimism	Hopeful
Neutrality	250	Trust	Satisfactory
Courage	**200**	**Affirmation**	**Feasible**
Pride	175	Scorn	Demanding
Anger	150	Hate	Antagonistic
Desire	125	Craving	Disappointing
Fear	100	Anxiety	Frightening
Grief	75	Regret	Tragic
Apathy	50	Despair	Hopeless
Guilt	30	Blame	Evil
Shame	20	Humiliation	Miserable

Source: Power Versus Force: An Anatomy of Consciousness, Dr. David Hawkins

Note: Column 1 heading changed from "Level" to "Feeling"; Column 2 heading changed from "Log" to "Truth" Measure, which is a logarithmic scale. [Hawkins used a Muscle Test on the arms of people to test for truth]. The "truth" measure could also be thought of as a scale of *emotional vibration*.

Manifesting desires, and the appropriate form of desires consistent with authentic living and awakened action, is the subject of Chapter 9: "Adventures." The feeling of gratitude, and reverence for all that-is, is considered very important and is the entire subject of Chapter 10.

Expanding the RAFTS Map

We need to expand on the components of the RAFTS Map in order to clarify the creative process of manifesting. The key thing here is the flow of joy into what we do and create.

Results	MANIFESTATIONS
Actions	
Feelings	
Thoughts	
State	
Map	

Mental Processes — BBB MAP → CC MAP ← D MAP — Imagination, Intuition, Inspiration, Insights, Ideas

Mind-Body Awareness/ "Being-ness" — AAAA MAP — True You

Another way of looking at the RAFTS Map using the time-tested gardening metaphor, is to view **State** as the Garden, the aspects connected to **Thoughts and Feelings** as Seeds, (presumably good, deliberate intentions although our involuntary ego or "monkey mind" can be tricky), and the Manifestations in terms of **Action** and **Results** as producing the flowers (or weeds).

Manifesting wisely is immensely important to all of us in leading a fulfilled and happy life. While what we want may sometimes be very clear to us, this is not always the case in navigating our lives, and introducing the above set of interlinked or integrated Maps helps us to be more explicit in **consciously determining what we want to manifest.**

The Maps that we will introduce as an expansion of the RAFTS Map are listed overleaf:

The AAAA Map: Awareness-Authenticity-Acceptance-Appreciation

The BBB Map: Beliefs to Behaviors to Benefits

The CC Map: Clarity and Commitment

The D Map: Destiny

Note that these expanded Maps of are part of life design. The Benefits and Behavior elements of the BBB Map, for example, are planning tools, and not necessarily the subsequent results and actions.

In expanding the RAFTS Map, we want to know that our goals are right for us, so they should come from our deeper authentic selves, and combine left and right brain mental processes to provide a holistic gestalt.

Let us now look at the AAAA, BBB, CC and D Maps in more detail.

CHAPTER 2

The AAAA Map: Awareness-Authenticity-Acceptance-Appreciation

A wareness of reality in the present moment leads to authenticity which in turn leads to acceptance and appreciation.

THE AAAA MAP — ALIGNING WITH TRUE SELF

Awareness
Here and Now
Ego Watching

Authenticity
Comfortable in own skin
Risk being yourself (vulnerable)

Acceptance
Compassion
Deep change

Appreciation
Gratitude
Growth

The four components of this Map are explained overleaf.

Awareness

Spirit, Life Force, Animus, Animating Presence, God, Universal Intelligence, Universal Mind, Universal Love, forever-Being, Big Mind

Humanity has been advised for thousands of years to live in the now, in the present. In conjunction with this, modern spiritual leaders such as Eckhart Tolle are advising us to be in touch with "Being," the spiritual side of us - if this seems like mumbo jumbo, just ask yourself whether most people would be aware of your spirit, (or life force or life energy), once you're dead! There must be something that makes us different from lifeless corpses!!

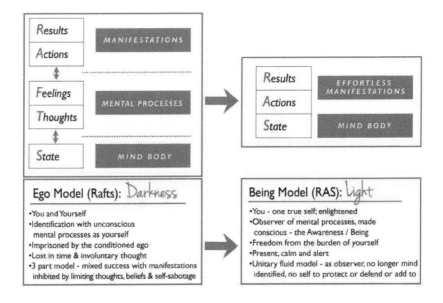

This recognition of forever-Being or Big Mind goes a stage beyond living in the now, to a state where we sense the life force itself. In this state, we are living in touch with the eternal, timeless, formless Big Mind (*Being* life force) in the present moment while the temporary form of Little Mind (*Human* ego) takes a relatively low place. There is a shift towards the Being Model (RAS).

In a fully awakened or enlightened person the ego might hardly be running at all. This is the opposite of the typical human condition where our frail ego forms are running our lives, so, for example, we *become* our anger, our resentment, our guilt or whatever emotion we are feeling at the time.

In awareness, as you learn to awaken to Being or Big Mind, you *observe* the thoughts and emotions that emanate from the ego, without identifying, judging, or getting caught up with them. As you awaken much more deeply, you experience your true nature in the present moment as the formless spacious stillness, the silence out of which forms (including thoughts and emotions) arise.

How do you enter the state of presence? It helps first to relax, to breathe deeply and then to divert your *attention* from your head into your body, (or you might choose to think of shifting attention from your head into your heart). Feel the inner body energy. Ideally, there will be gaps in thinking, (yet without consciously resisting thought), referred to as "no-mind" in the East. This helps to clear mental noise or clutter, while at the same time opens you up to the far greater intelligence of the universe, well beyond that of little mind or your ego thought streams. Your body has intelligence well beyond your mind, something which your mind knows nothing of. It is this intelligence that creative people like Albert Einstein have drawn upon. When you are **fully present in the now** you can feel Oneness with all that is, with Being or Big Mind – you sense enlightenment.

Enlightened beings know that humans have free will, and that the vulnerable, self-protective ego, the fearful ego, the ego-possessed little mind running amok, has caused and continues to cause havoc on our planet. (Think of World Wars, Civil Wars, and countless millions that died for ideologies in Russia, China and Cambodia, etc.). Awareness is evidently important to our sanity and survival as a species.

The state of the world reflects the present state of evolution of human beings. Hopefully the challenges that the humans experience from their fearful ego will in time give way to a more benign consciousness or awareness. (In connection therewith, human development is relatively young. Some scientists believe that human language, and by inference ego, commenced around 50,000 years ago. In comparison some scientists believe that that the earth is circa 4.5 billion years old and that the universe is circa 13.8 billion years old. But, perhaps we don't really know – maybe the universe has always been here. It is just beyond human intelligence to understand how incredible amounts of energy came into the universe, in contradiction to the scientific observation that energy cannot be created (only transformed).

We need to remember the limitations of little mind. Consider that we wouldn't expect an ant to understand the human mind, so why should we expect the human mind to fully comprehend Universal Mind or God? As an aside, perhaps Jesus' assertion that we can only reach God through him was symbolic as we can all relate to Jesus, (and other luminaries too), but cannot relate directly to the God that we cannot see, other than, through our background awareness.

Authenticity: Showing Up as True Self

Stemming from your awareness, the higher awareness/ spirit/ life force/ Big Mind, is your timeless source essence that flows into everything that you think, feel and do. You only have to remind yourself to be present in this very moment, to observe and quiet your mind, in order to sense the ever-present background silence, stillness and spaciousness that you are.

This may sound a bit fanciful, yet let's face it the whole of existence is arguably beyond belief. This universe, (or multiverse), that we are integral with, and not separate from, is an incredible marvel of perhaps infinite energy that we tend to forget or take for granted as we go about our day to day mind-concerns. And this is even more incredible given "proof" from rigorous science that energy can neither be created nor destroyed. If this was always true the Universe could not exist. The whole world is your garden - it belongs to you as much as anyone else - well you can look at it anyway!

It is in the very nature of aware authentic people to live in a state of love, joy and gratitude; knowing that they are already whole, complete, and good enough; that more than that, they are an expression of eternal awareness, of the universe's life energy. And whereas little mind/ ego in most humans is running their lives, keeping them fearful and small, increasing numbers of people are learning to live through spirit/ life force/ Big Mind giving expression of that life force to benefit the environments in which they operate.

Authentic people know who they are, know how all humans are, and learn to recognize unconsciousness with compassion, should it arise in themselves or others. They have learned to be comfortable in their own skin and to risk being themselves; as the false, time-bound, conditioned cloak of ego, gives way to the reality of being in the present, in the here and now, this very moment.

Authentic, aware beings are calm, they clear their little mind/ ego and operate from beyond – in stillness, silence, spaciousness, from Big Mind. They have learned to be wary of the ego surreptitiously creeping in to justify certain mental positions, or view-points, that the mind identifies with, and wishes to defend.

Since the creative spirit/ life force/ love energy is flowing through them, authentic beings sufficiently exposed to the light of awareness have only love and abundance to give – for them living is giving, this is their nature.

Acceptance: Non-resistance to What-is; Powerful Change through Presence, forever-Being

Acceptance is a major factor in *freedom* from the psychological pain that we feel when our ego reacts and argues with what-is, wishing it to be different from the current reality. Accepting and surrendering to what-is; living without clingy attachments; letting go; and dis-identifying with negative thoughts and emotions. In truly full acceptance, nothing will faze you, you have nothing to fear – the ultimate strength. And in this "State," you have more clarity to enjoy the fullness of life, to expand your capacity to live in joy, and to have some fun in life! No need to take things too seriously.

Acceptance is not condoning or being resigned to an unacceptable situation; it is being calm and collected, compassionate where people are involved and appropriately responsive. Any knee-jerk reaction, inner tension or frustration is a sure sign of the anxious, fearful ego, although prompt and assertive action may be necessary in some circumstances. With a clear mind, indeed operating from the perspective of Big Mind, you can come up with effective solutions and purposeful change.

Enlightened beings accept and surrender to what-is, and paradoxically this is their strength. They stay present, (rather than being lost in past or future save for conscious, voluntary, practical purposes), and are creative when challenges arise, enabling the life energy of Being to operate through them. (Jesus – I of myself do nothing ...).

It's the reactive resistant mind that creates stress in our lives; the reactive little mind that resists what-is and creates all manner of anxious, distressful thoughts and emotions around it – fearing, blaming, and complaining. Enlightened beings learn to accept what-is without resistance; yet they will still honor their preferences, follow their wishes, and follow their hearts. And, they will make effective and powerful changes for the better guided by Being or Big Mind.

Do you have to accept bad things that happen to you? No, complaint may be valid, yet errors are drawn to attention without anger or blame; a mistake has been made and it needs resolution – that's all.

Do you have to accept all the terrible things that the media feeds us with on a daily basis? No, you may feel grateful for your comparative good fortune, you may benefit if your "dark side" is operating, or you may choose not to read, watch or listen.

Alternatively, your attention to news media may make you aware of a cause for which you can really make a difference. If so, then go ahead and contribute what you can – the world needs you! Yet you are not necessarily here to solve any of the world's major challenges – only to participate in the flow of life, contributing harmoniously, according to your particular talents, aspirations and any calling that you feel from within.

Appreciation: Growth and Gratitude

Appreciation includes *growth* and *gratitude*. Big mind is for growth, the evolution of human beings and all life, and we can tap into intuition, connect and "download" from Big Mind/ Universal Mind/ Being. Big Mind is totally abundant. Now this may sound a bit far-fetched, yet most of the limitations in life are self-imposed through thoughts arising from our ego, that react to conditions of the particular era and environment into which we were born. If you're not feeling lucky and blessed by life, just decide to be lucky from today by making a decision to love what-is, and perhaps live life as a Spiritual Warrior, defeating your inner ego related (or "shadow-self") demons.

We are all one with source – we all came from the same place – all forged from the same elements – all *interdependent* and *inter-being* with the sun, the earth, the oceans, the air and space. Furthermore, we are all *impermanent* and in cosmic terms, our lives are less than a cosmic second!! Gratitude for our brief sojourn on Earth is fundamental. You are meant to live in a *State* of love, joy and gratitude, bringing acceptance, enjoyment or enthusiasm to all your endeavors. Let not the cultural conditioning of society detract from your happiness!! Break free today!

In the table shown overleaf, we further highlight general differences in tendencies between living from the perspective of ego or forever-Being.

Ego Characteristics	Being Characteristics
Non Awareness	**Awareness**
Buffeted and swayed by involuntary thoughts and emotions of the ego as they pop-up.	Living in the here and now as forever-Being and witness of the mind – thoughts and emotions – without attachment.
Assumes a heavy mantle of self that is entirely separate from everything else.	One with all that is. Connected through billions of ancestors to Source/ God/ life.
The heavy drapes of conditioned ego obscure the light of consciousness. Imprisoned...	"Light of the world" beyond the opaque screen of conditioned ego; sense "the kingdom of heaven within." Freedom ...
Non-Authenticity	**Authenticity**
Conformist and slave to conditioning and whims of others; keeping up with the Jones's; living in lack; ruled by unconscious thoughts and emotions; too vulnerable to be vulnerable to others; not comfortable with oneself; feels incomplete; too self-absorbed to help others.	Living life on one's own terms; meets own needs; living with a sense of abundance; living consciously and forging one's own life; strong minded; comfortable in own skin. Whole, complete and enough. Warm appreciation for life. Lives to give. Motto: I'm here for you.
Non-Acceptance	**Acceptance**
Stress from continually judging, resisting and reacting to "what-is;" inability to let go of the past; fearful of a projected future. Unduly upset when things don't go as expected. Unnecessarily pre-occupied with other people's business.	Befriends the Present Moment with warm acceptance. Calm, yet bold in the face of "what-is." "Doesn't mind what happens." Intelligent responses to situations as opposed to knee-jerk reactions. Gives compassion and forgiveness for human unconsciousness – "they know not what they do." Non-judgmental. Surrendered to the Sunshine, not apathy.
Non-Appreciation	**Appreciation**
Takes everything for granted; blind to blessings; focused on the bad rather than the good; experiences stagnation; inability to grow and move forward; victim and blame oriented; excuse oriented.	Feeling good about blessings; hopeful for the future, yet living and enjoying the moment and journey without undue preoccupation with results; focused on growth appropriate to life phase, life situation, strengths and personal values.

I recall reading a book by a renowned coach in which it was stated that in life there is just "You" and "IT" with IT referring to our life situation - events and other people. That resonated with me at the time and is correct at one level, yet there is a tendency to see "you" from the perspective of the ego rather than true self. In awareness, we observe our thoughts and emotions rather than becoming them, being identified with them, or being possessed by them.

THE JOURNEY FROM EGO TO AWARENESS TO PURE CONSCIOUSNESS MAP

The (non-judgmental, present moment), Stage 1 *awareness* referred to in this Map is beyond thought. In present moment awareness, or observation of our ego and life, a new dimension of consciousness has come in. Observing the ego is to be a silent witness of our thoughts and emotions or feelings. You are not your perceptions per se – sensory or mental – but the observer. You do not need to follow *every* thought, like a dog following scent, especially negative ones borne out of fearful ego.

Could it be that your *awareness* is tied to your *forever-Being,* and to the *life force* that separates you from your corpse, in a continuous thread back through your billions of ancestors to original Source? Go inside and ask "Who am I?" and see what comes up for you.

In Stage 2 of the above Map, your life force is sensed as being one with the divine without separation. According to Ajahn Brahm, a Cambridge University educated Buddhist monk, writing in The Art of Disappearing – The Buddha's path to Lasting Joy, "The whole path becomes one of gradual vanishing."

The *ego* is an antennae constantly looking out for threats to our well-being and this is both natural, and to some extent necessary, given the vulnerable form of human beings born into this world. If we didn't have fear we might not live very long! When that voice in our head says let that truck pass before crossing the road it's quite right. While acting on our perceptions can keep us safe, it's worth noting that our intelligence and sensory abilities are limited, and we can know this by observing the perceptions of other life forms, for example, in terms of ranges of sight, hearing and spatial awareness. As mentioned earlier, our lives are very short, if we're lucky 100 years, a speck in comparison to the life of Planet Earth, yet long compared to a mosquito with longevity typically only a few days for some male species. When you're an 8 year old human being, 100 years looks so far off it's not worth considering. If our typical life span was closer to 20 years perhaps we would all think and behave differently.

In contrast, *forever-Being* is essentially fearless because life is forever, unlimited. We cannot claim to be the *Creator* – we are the *created* in common with all other life forms. As human beings we can be a bit skeptical about our origins and any future beyond our current human form, yet we take for granted this incredible, perhaps timeless universe, of perhaps limitless energy. We are oblivious to this incredible phenomenon most of the time, because it is so familiar like the air that we breathe and it doesn't pose a direct threat to us. We may sense or get a glimpse of it on a rare, still, silent occasion of solitude or with our lover, gazing into the starry night. Yet, we were formed from that same incredible Source. Is it such a stretch to believe that this life force in us, that separates us from our corpse, is actually part of the formless Source expressing itself?

We need a *shift* from *conditioned unconsciousness* to *non-conditioned consciousness.* In the shift from *conditioned* to *non-conditioned* we move from habitual ingrained thought patterns to seeing with a "beginner's mind," dropping pre-conceived notions and assumptions about the way things are. In the shift from *unconsciousness* to *consciousness* we move from automatic pilot to conscious, deliberate creation. In "Pure Awareness," the ultimate stage of awareness entered into by mystics, we are one with the Creator and the objects of our awareness – everything is sacred. Ego and (forever) Being is contrasted in more detail overleaf.

EGO Characteristics	BEING Characteristics
Non Awareness	**Awareness**
Separate self, emotional baggage, survival	Background stillness, spaciousness; flow
Identified with mind created dramas	Dis-identified from mind created dramas
Confusion & illusion of *past and future*	Living in clarity and reality in the *present*
Jeopardy, suffering; good and bad cycles	Joy (non-polarized)
Conditioned, unconscious, form-identity	Non-conditioned, conscious, soulful
Hijacked by issues, problems	Nothing is *felt* as a problem
Becoming important, more than	Realized true Self, that's important!
Little Mind (limitations, bondage)	Big Mind (freedom)
Non-Authenticity	**Authenticity**
Incomplete, lacking	Complete
Inadequate	Good enough
Anxious, disturbed and fearful	Bold, calm and fearless
Express negativity	Express love, joy and gratitude
Problem absorbed	Decision and action oriented
Unwise choices and decisions	Wise choices and decisions
Self-centered, me and mine	Contributing to many, sharing, giving
Left brain tendencies (excessively so)	Right brain & heart expressed tendencies
Non-Acceptance	**Acceptance**
Resists what-is & feels stress; reactionary	Accept what-is: calm & adaptable
Judgmental & self-righteous	Non-judgmental: solution-oriented
Clingy, needy	Non-attachment: equanimity
Tense physiology	Relaxed physiology
Resentful, vengeful	Forgiving
Imprisoned in negative cycles	Free, unfettered agent of deep change
Non-Appreciation	**Appreciation**
Complaining, blaming, victimhood	Realizing your creative capacities
Paying attention to what's not right	Paying attention to the good in your life
Failure to take 100% responsibility for life no matter what happens	100% responsibility for *your one and precious life*. Health, wealth and happiness!
Familiarity has led to blindness to the miracles of life	Appreciates the miracles of the Universe, nature, modernization and life

CHAPTER 3

The BBB Map: Beliefs-Behaviors-Benefits

This Map helps us to question and generate or modify our **B**eliefs and **B**ehaviors, in order to provide or manifest **B**enefits in alignment with Big Mind or Being, the life energy that flows through all of us, albeit obscured by ego and lack of presence to a lesser or greater degree.

THE BBB MAP: ALIGNING BELIEFS, BEHAVIORS AND BENEFITS/ RESULTS

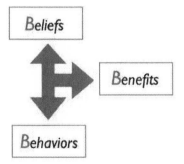

The Map starts from the premise that many beliefs are not rock-solid, and indeed, often-times aren't true at all! Little mind-ego is inclined as a temporary form to sense lack – not good enough, not deserving enough, not loved enough, not important enough, not respected enough, not admired enough, not rich enough – the list is potentially endless! No wonder that human beings possessed by little mind are inclined to suffer! Time to move over to Big Mind or forever-Being!! And, let go of that heavy, little mind persona baggage.

With little mind running the show, it is easy to pick up all sorts of erroneous limiting conditioning and beliefs, as we grow up in our particular environment on this Planet Earth. And, of course, we are vulnerable – just one false move crossing the road and kaput! Born a prince or a pauper, we are prone to limiting conditioning and beliefs that impinge on our freedom as human beings.

If you were born in Italy you may have picked up the cultural conditioning of your country and the beliefs of Catholics; similarly in India the beliefs of Hindus; and in Indonesia, of Moslems. This is a wider conditioning; then we have our ancestral roots, pre-dating religions that might be surprisingly common; and we have the more specific conditioning from our families, schools and so on that shape our early beliefs.

Some of our most important beliefs can be categorized under "wheel of life" themes, beliefs about managing our relationships, health, money, leisure, career and so on. Beliefs can also be classified under what we value most dearly in our day to day lives– our "values."

Let's get on to application of the BBB Map then. In order to experience the benefit of a great relationship, for example, our behaviors, especially what we do and say, need to be responsive to the needs of the other person and our beliefs must be congruent with our behaviors. Rather than go into a lot of dialogue about beliefs, behaviors and benefits, the table commencing overleaf illustrates the "BBB Map" in action. In this table the benefits are related to personal values such as Freedom, Love, Adventure, Gratitude and Service (FLAGS). The beliefs part of us can be more closely aligned with ego/ little mind or Being/ Big Mind. There is evidence to suggest that the more closely we are aligned with forever-Being, the more fulfilled we are likely to be in our lives and this is related to the potentially insatiable appetite of the ego for more, more, more!!

BELIEFS ... KNOWING	BEHAVIORS	BENEFITS
Our huge, miraculous universe comprises <u>One</u> indivisible, creative, infinite, eternal, source energy or <u>life force</u> arising from beyond the "Big Bang." (Introduction refers).	Feel <u>warm appreciation</u> for the awesome miracle of life. Stay in touch with the sacredness of life: forgotten when living from the human mind's perception of lack.	FREEDOM ...from ego, the heavy burden of self, lost in time, fear & mind-created illusion...
This <u>life force</u>/ spirit/ Big Mind/ universal intelligence/ <u>consciousness in you</u> and in everything is formless, eternal & timeless. "I Am that I Am."	Feel spaciousness, stillness, silence and expansiveness in the Now, in the flow of life; relaxed and surrendered to what-is without resistance.	...from imperfect conditioning & habits, conformity, and society-based role identity
You're not running the show here on Planet Earth.	Get out of your own way! Let go of some expectations.	Needless stress will be minimized
You were created, possibly did not ask to be born, and you are not the thoughts and emotions that come and go.	Feel <u>Aware</u>. Face and examine thoughts and emotions; identify with Joyous true Self, not mind-based anxieties.	An unblocked mind allows the creative life force to flow thru' you
All forms are transient, impermanent. Your lifespan is less than a cosmic second!	Feel <u>Bold, Calm</u> and <u>Detached</u> anchored in the Now without clingy or fearful attachments.	A relatively carefree life not bound to ongoing drama
As forever-Being, you will outlive your temporary human form.	Feel relatively unconcerned with comings and goings. And observe nature ...	More joy! And wisdom
We are all expressions of the one indivisible life energy. One with Life.	Express your whole life from the Joy of eternal forever-Being.	LOVE ... a warm appreciation for all
We are all inter-being with everything else yet at different levels of consciousness.	Give forgiveness, acceptance, compassion, empathy & support to yourself & others.	Less judgmental of ourselves and others
Less conscious people are more impacted by challenges due to high ego-needs and conditioned attachments.	Give without expecting return; try to raise consciousness so that people can be less needy and help themselves.	Happier and more fruitful lives

BELIEFS ... KNOWING	BEHAVIORS	BENEFITS
Life is this moment, Now, indulging our God-given senses. Look! Listen! Feel! Life is love and there is no need to let fear hold us back. Life *is* change & transformation.	Live, love, experience every moment fearlessly, (assuming there's no tiger in the room). Live moments in situations of your choosing. Live moments with joy & enthusiasm.	ADVENTURES ... Great moments!
We live in an awesome abundant universe of infinite, free energy & our ancestors have co-created modern civilization, cultures, environments that we can enjoy.	Feel good about your blessings every day Feel good about perfection, beauty & miracles without overly labelling & judging.	GRATITUDE ... for so many things to feel good about
Contributing to life is part of the essence of being human, a natural expression of Joy & creative energy emanating from our Creator, flowing through us & returning to Source in a continuous loop.	Contribute through: Lifelong learning & skill development. Helping to provide products, projects or services that best express your talents & resources, while benefiting others. Funding of causes that aim to eliminate suffering.	SERVICE ... contribution and a sense of influence, usefulness and progress

"Being" is also about increase ... indeed, many scientists believe that our awesome, incomprehensibly vast universe is expanding ... yet Being-related increase is selfless rather than selfish.

While the BBB Map generally flows logically from beliefs to behaviors to benefits, other permutations are possible as described overleaf.

Behaviors to Benefits to Beliefs

In this mode, we learn from our *behaviors*. Indeed, this is how we formed many of our beliefs in the first place, and sometimes rooted in positive or negative reinforcement from family, teachers, peers and so on. In organizational settings, this mode has long been recognized as a means to inculcate beliefs through personal experience, rather than attempting to change beliefs directly, (which can be more challenging).

Behavior then, is an important starting point for generating beliefs and change. The difference between super-successful people and everyone else often boils down to their rituals or habits. These can include:

- Developing an effective mind-set
- Diet, exercise and sleep routines
- Paying more attention to our physiology and posture
- Learning new skills
- Paying attention to the environments in which we place ourselves

Great rituals lead to great results. Sloppy habits lead to sloppy results. It's that simple. While simple, oftentimes we are stuck in our current habitual patterns in our day to day living. Moreover, for many of us, it is not easy to change to more effective habits that serve us and others better. Practices for changing habits are covered in Chapter 12.

If you were lucky, you may have grown up with some good role models that helped you to establish really good habits. If not, it's never too late. While you can learn from studies in personal development, your progress can be accelerated by associating with the right people that may include formal mentors or coaches.

The most important habits come under mind-set, especially developing a spiritual mind-set compatible with forever-Being, and ultimately this is what will provide the most fulfillment. Developing awareness, slowing and reconditioning automatic thinking, self-observation, accepting what-is, practicing forgiveness, compassion and gratitude are prime examples of habits conducive to forever-Being. Related thereto, it makes sense to ensure that your values contain elements consistent with forever-Being.

It would be a shame in our old age to regret that we didn't really live! Any assessment of our lives depends on how we think, and ultimately it could be a realization "oh, no, I need to do rather better in the next life!" Some might take a more relaxed approach and conclude that if we are "forever-Being," then it's more a case of "never mind, I've got plenty of time to get it right!"

Our fulfillment depends on our progression towards achieving worthy ideals - including of course, living in accordance with our values. Will the rewards outweigh the efforts? This is something that each of us needs to weigh-up. If along with our efforts we can maintain energy and happiness we are doing well.

Benefits to Behaviors to Beliefs

In this mode we start by considering the *benefits* desired, and then ask what *beliefs* we would need to have in place, in order to manifest the required behaviors and benefits. Of course, such beliefs have to be believable, so it's necessary to find appropriate logic and experience that supports the beliefs under consideration.

Note that this approach differs from the "Beliefs to Behaviors to Benefits" approach that we first considered. In that mode, we started with beliefs or knowing things that are already apparent, albeit based on potentially new perspectives.

The approach being taken here, can be framed as "what do I need to believe or become in order to manifest the reality I am seeking?" This generally requires working on ourselves to change limiting beliefs and become what we want to be, in order to make our desires come true. Making a decision to awaken to forever-Being, for example, by becoming a "Spiritual Warrior" or a "Buddha," would help you to overcome your ego and live a more fulfilled life. Some characteristics of alpha males (or females) may also be worthy of emulating.

A great thing for anyone wanting to become a Spiritual Warrior is that it can be achieved in an instant, through a simple decision and commitment to overcoming your demons. This is analogous in some respects to becoming a golfer, where you commit to both reducing your handicap, and improving your performance, simultaneously. Pointers on how to live as a Spiritual Warrior are provided in Chapter 9: "Adventures."

CHAPTER 4

The CC Map: Clarity and Commitment

While the foregoing BBB Map showed the incredible source of power available to you according to your beliefs, the simple CC Map depicted below concerns harnessing the power of Clarity and Commitment to keep you on track.

THE CC MAP: SOLIDIFYING CLARITY AND COMMITMENT

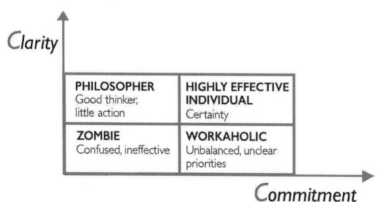

The worst case scenario with reference to the boxes of the CC Map is to behave like a Zombie. Lack of goal clarity goes hand in hand with lack of commitment, and the result is confusion and ineffectiveness.

It is difficult to commit to a course of action if we're not clear about that which we want to manifest. We might have too many choices and lack the skills to evaluate the best way forward. We may need to ask ourselves new questions, improve access to information, rely on intuition or seek out suitable mentors to improve clarity.

In the case of the Philosopher, there may be keen clarity on what needs to be achieved, and a very intelligent analysis of the pros and cons on the way forward, yet somehow there is no commitment to action. There could be any number of reasons for this including a conflict with personal values, fear of getting it wrong, lack of faith or confidence, pride in intellectual prowess, a feeling of being outside one's comfort zone, and potential losses of reputation, funds, etc.

Workaholics may appear to be highly committed, but committed to what? By definition, workaholics are unfulfilled. There is a lack of balance in handling their "wheel of life" – particular aspects of relationships, career, finances, relaxation, and health and so on. It may be that the workaholic is seeking distraction from painful aspects of a life situation or is ego-obsessed in proving his or her self-worth. Workaholics may be so caught up in themselves that they miss out on life. We are not referring here to people who really love what they are doing, and some people may be happily unbalanced from time to time!

The sweet-spot of course is the *Highly Effective Individual,* who is both clear on goals, and committed to appropriate action. There is *Clarity* on what one really, really wants as well as the determined *Commitment* to achieve or manifest it. A fusion of these two aspects means that you have *made up your mind*, pure and simple. It will happen and nothing is going to prevent it - there is no "Plan B" and all other bridges have been burnt!!

There is nothing to beat *a made up mind.* Rather than reflecting rigid, "egoism" and stubbornness, a made up mind may be regarded as a noble, even spiritual quality, provided it stems from complete authenticity. And with a made up mind there is no way that quitting will happen.

In a quote frequently attributed to Goethe and to WH Murray, it is suggested that "until one has committed, there is hesitancy, the chance to draw back... whatever you do, or dream you can do, begin it. Boldness has genius, power and magic in it. Begin it now!"

Let us look now at how some well-known personalities from the fields of business, sports and acting who have achieved notable levels of success in the context of goal clarity and commitment.

Arnold Schwarzenegger: *Have a clear goal and do whatever it takes to get there! Believe in yourself; work your butt off*

Sylvester Stallone: Keep moving forward – that's how winning is done! *Find your process; do one thing right*

Bruce Lee: *Commit fearlessly!*

Will Smith: *Commit! Be amazing at what you do; don't be outworked!*

Donald Trump: *Never, ever give up; be totally focused; work hard*

Steve Jobs: *Build vision-inspired teams; have passion and do what you love; design for yourself*

Tim Ferris: *Have 1 or 2 focused weekly metrics; focus on your strengths; use failure to help you*

Warren Buffet: *Schedule for your personality, find your passion, give unconditional love*

Bill Gates: *Work hard; have energy, create the future*

Hard Work or Effortless Manifestation?

It's interesting to see the references to hard work. What happened to the "effortless manifestation" suggested by many Law of Attraction promoters, with resources lining up in alignment with our thoughts as broadcast out to the universe? In Chapter 1, in introducing the RAFTS Map, we referred to the possibility of "synchronicities" or helpful coincidences, and Jung's "collective consciousness," and suggested that you make up your own mind based on your experiences.

Then, at the beginning of Chapter 2, we showed the RAFTS Map simplified to RAS – Results, Actions, and State - implying that from the perspective of forever-Being, fleeting thoughts and feelings associated with needs of the ego carry no weight at all. We referred to RAS as a "unitary fluid Map – as observer, no longer mind identified no self to protect, defend or add to," so that our thoughts and actions stem from a bigger picture perspective.

What is this bigger picture perspective? Well, it is not tainted by ego, me and mine, and I'll be happy when ...., and it is what comes out from whatever shifts are necessary to live in Awareness, Authenticity, Acceptance and Appreciation – the AAAA Map of Chapter 2. This varies from person to person according to their present place on the path. In Chapter 7 on Freedom, we introduce the SHIFT Map which draws on some core elements of the AAAA Map that we need to focus on to live a happier and more fulfilled life. Who knows, this may eventually lead to effortless manifestations, yet we will need to do a lot of work on ourselves to make the shift. On the other hand this may be a labor of love and the rewards divine.

There appears to be adequate empirical evidence that "committing fearlessly" as Bruce Lee puts it, does indeed invoke the law of attraction and the people and resources to keep moving us forward.

Bill Gates cites the core importance of energy. If we have the energy, then it's not hard work unless our heart really isn't in it. So building our energy is something that we can focus on physically, (exercise, diet, quality sleep, etc.), and spiritually, (through oneness with the flow of Source energy, presence and surrender, etc.). Interestingly, Warren Buffet cites unconditional love as a key element in worldly success and clarifies that passion isn't about doubling, quadrupling, etc., but tied to meaning.

In Chapter 9, we provide a quote by the late Alan Watts, a famous spiritual teacher who suggests that we regard work as play which sounds rather like effortless manifestation. I guess it depends on what sort of work it is, how it was designed and the environment in which it's carried out, as these will impact our ability to see the element of play. But, what Alan Watts as a spiritual teacher is suggesting of course, is that we bring our *true self* to the work place so that we can live it in a different way – a happier and more productive one with the potential for better relationships and results. And one can imagine that if both job designers and implementers carried an enlightened attitude, then workplaces would be transformed.

In Chapter 11 we introduce the value of Service, which is about *how* we do what we choose to do, and advocate focus on the process (activity set) rather than the pre-defined result, and employing mindfulness to savor the doing in the moment. So focusing on process rather than stressing outcomes will make work more enjoyable.

Vision Inspired Teams

As the late Steve Jobs advocates, a vision that catches fire throughout an organization, including its individual organizational units and teams, will engender both clarity and commitment. It lends to the development of a high performance (work) culture when coupled with other elements such as *simplicity*, another cornerstone of Jobs' philosophy.

Persistence

As Donald Trump has learned from his experience, we need to *maintain momentum* and avoid getting side tracked by unnecessary distractions. Schwarzenegger suggests to "do whatever it takes to get there!" And, Stallone enthuses us to "Keep moving forward – that's how winning is done!" Interestingly life-coach Robin Sharma also promotes "KMF," (Keep Moving Forward), as a slogan for maintaining persistence.

Never the less, a caveat needs to be added to the subject of persistence. One needs to remain open and flexible to responding to unforeseen changes in circumstances or the emergence of vital new information that might cause us to question our goal or our approach to achieving it. On the other hand we need to avoid mere excuses or unfounded procrastination. In the latter case we need to evaluate the cause and potential limiting beliefs and fears.

In many circumstances, the high level mission, vision and values remain sacrosanct, while lower level goals, tasks and tactics are accorded more flexibility, commensurate with the changing day to day situation or operating environment.

Task Scheduling to Engender Commitment

Motivated by the fact that, at least presently, I'm not a "morning person," I would like to add a few words in-keeping with Buffet's advice on scheduling. This entails committing to your goals at the times that are right for you. So you don't have to get up at 5am in the morning as some life-coaches suggest, unless, of course, that's your preference which is fine; the key point is that you *do* have to commit significant time to working on your goals during the hours that are convenient for you and, if feasible, this will coincide with the time(s) of the day when you feel at your best. In Chapter 12, we draw attention to the important productivity habit of "time blocking" that helps us to maintain commitment.

In order for the odds to be absolutely stacked in your favor, goals must be meaningful and deemed well worth the effort. And, remember that the journey, the step that you take right now, is important too. Recall also that "the road to hell is paved with good intentions," which is the way of the non-authentic and selective ego! In order to avoid this road, the "1D" Map described in the following chapter helps us to adopt an authentic path in realizing our destiny.

CHAPTER 5

The D Map: Destiny

T he "D" in this Map represents Destiny, Dream, Direction, or Destination, forged in the quiet present moment of stillness, with access to Big Mind (or Being/ Universal Intelligence/ God, Universal Love, etc.), as opposed to the fearful voice of ego.

THE D MAP: DESTINY AND LIFE DESIGN

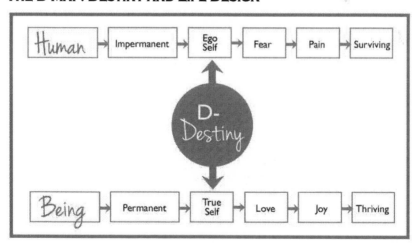

With reference to the 1D Map, our Destiny can be motivated from fear and pain, or flow naturally from a powerful State of Being. That said, suffering can be a great teacher, if and when, challenging life situations arise, and may be a very necessary part of our growth.

It is assumed that when we pass away, the human form no longer exists other than dust ultimately, while the life force, the forever-Being, (the difference between your current self and your corpse), an energy that cannot be destroyed, transforms, becoming our next mysterious adventure. Now which side of us should we nurture, the permanent forever-Being side or the impermanent human side? The Map suggests that we need to take care that, as far as possible, our Destiny is aligned with our permanent True Self, rather than our impermanent Ego Self.

This is consistent with the statement of Russell E. Dicarlo writing in the preface to Eckhart Tolle's book "The Power of NOW," (Hodder and Stoughton 2005 edition), that "our ultimate *destiny* is to re-connect with our essential Being and express from our extraordinary, divine reality in the ordinary physical world, moment by moment." That is to say we need to manifest from our eternal state of forever-Being or True Self rather than from our time-bound state of conditioned ego.

Things and conditions may provide us with pleasure, yet these are often temporary. The new home, the new car, the new degree award may thrill us for a week or two! That said, if you have arranged your life well – vocation, partner, family, home, car, environment, etc. – and you are doing things that you enjoy, then you have much to be grateful for on a regular basis. And I'm not knocking a good education that may be a necessary prerequisite for a glorious career or any of the material things mentioned. If you really want something, then go get it! So long as you're not staking your future happiness on its achievement because you may find the pleasure quite short lived, and time wasted has gone forever. "Oh, I've got that now but I still feel a bit empty! There's still something missing, and something more I need, before I can really feel fulfilled!" On the other hand, it does make sense to create a financial "nest egg" early on, to free yourself from financial pressures later in life. This can give you both time, as well as financial freedom, which are potentially very precious if used wisely.

Our choices in life should provide us with joy while contributing to the whole - all life. This really suggests that our primary purpose is to operate from forever-Being as True Self as much as possible, manifesting relatively effortlessly from that State of Being according to our heart's desires. It is generally recognized that our main choices in life concern *being, doing,* and *having* (or acquiring). Consistent with the 1D Map, forever-Being is the most important. Before we "decide" what to do and have, we need to know who we are. Once that we are clear on who we are – *discovered, realized* our true selves as forever-Being – then decisions about the doing and having should become easier. Seeing through the eyes of forever-Being, you will make better and happier choices.

Realize deeply that you are already enough, whole and complete, and that pursuing a destiny is just a game that you choose to play, and since you happen to be here on Planet Earth for a short time, you might as well do something worthwhile. You are happy now, not when the next (of many) goals are accomplished. Living this way, you can be at peace just about always, and happy most of the time.

Working Out What You Want in Life

The *only* time that you can change your direction or destiny is now, this very moment. Factors that you may want to consider are:

1. Your State of Consciousness and Wellbeing
2. Your Wheel of Life
3. Making your Mark (Your One Thing)
4. Your Values
5. Your Strengths
6. Your Preferences
7. A systematic process for planning and executing your goals

Item 1 is about the major theme of this book – creating from a higher state of consciousness and with your wellbeing, happiness and authenticity as top priority.

Item 2 is about life themes that impact your wellbeing such as health, wealth, family and friends, career, romantic relationships, and hobbies, personal development and the physical environment

Item 3 is about having a purpose and making a difference. What's your one thing?

Item 4 is about what's important to you – such as freedom, love, etc.

Item 5 is about identifying and employing your signature strengths – and don't necessarily assume you know what these are – take tests to find out; ask friends for feedback; delegate to others in areas your less good at

Item 6 is about knowing your preferences – such as your thinking and learning styles and choice of life pursuits

Item 7 can make use of strategic planning maps that take you from here to there by means of a *strategy* that steers you through *challenges* to achieve your vision, mission and objectives. A related technique is the "4D" Map developed by the author covering Diagnosis, Destination, and Design and Doing; the latter refers to execution of an Action Plan derived from the (life) design stage of this map.

Goals versus "No Needs"

If our spiritual quest recognizes that we are already whole and complete, good enough, and have all the love we need inside of us already, then you might question the necessity of goals. The fact is that we humans are innately goal directed from the time that we arise, otherwise we might choose to sleep all day, and clearly most of us do not choose to do that on a regular basis if at all. Aside from that, our happiness is bound to contributing something and being of service during our sojourn on Planet Earth. Indeed, research has confirmed that our main opportunity to control our happiness lies in our life choices and activities. And this is pretty much self-evident.

Some related thoughts:
- You were created by your Creator for a purpose
- Your life energy or creative life force needs expression
- Consider that there is a feedback loop from your Creator to you (the created), to the world and back to the Creator

- Well as you're here anyway, you might as well do something worthwhile with your God-given talents! And, especially if this supports your wellbeing and fullness of life and helps others

Other than a roof over your head, food and drink, and some clothing suited to your environment there isn't much else you *really* need is there? It's only your conditioned psychological needs that have the potential to drive you nuts until such time that you realize that you need to get out of your own way and go with the flow. Yet as Eckhart Tolle advises, (as the consciousness of forever-Being), we can enjoy playing with form – not because we need to, but because we enjoy it. And, in doing so, we engage our God-given senses, that we received to enjoy things in moderation, and not just for survival. The qualification of "in moderation" is important. As you may have recognized from personal experience, the "law of diminishing returns" sets in whenever we over-indulge our senses be it sleeping, staying awake, eating, sex, listening to music, watching TV, etc.

In the context of goals and needs, spiritual masters offer various suggestions:
- Non-attachment to results (Buddha)
- Resolve inner purpose then enjoy playing with form (Tolle)
- I don't mind what happens (Khrishnamurti)
- Loving what-is (Byron Katie)
- Living in gratitude (all spiritual masters)

Getting What You Want – Faith and Belief

According to Jesus, whenever you ask for something, believe that you have received it, and it will be given to you. We could define a belief as a thought that you feel to be true. In order to manifest your desire, feel it to be true that you already have it, then hold on to that feeling and whatever comes up for you such as images and feelings. Note that you really have to believe, otherwise it doesn't work, so Jesus advises "according to your faith it is done unto you." Coming from the perspective of forever-Being, which implies truth, faith, good vibrations, intuition and no-needs you can create more readily as shown in the contrasted RAFTS and RAS Maps in Chapter 2.

If you employ affirmations such as "I'm a millionaire" when your net worth is negative, this may not feel (vibrate) right and fail to produce results. In order to overcome such dis-belief and resultant self-sabotage Noah St. John advises to engage in self-talk questions such as "why am I so rich?" This stimulates the mind-body to come up with positive thoughts, feelings and actions that align with the question. In this particular case, the mind may come up with non-monetary sources of richness or abundance.

And, again with reference to Jesus, "it is the father who doeth the works." The Creator, the Source, works through us, the created ones. Life flows from the Creator as it has always done, and continues to do in every moment, across, quite possibly, countless Universes and countless life forms. We are co-creators, manifesting desires using our free-will, while the life-energy of Source works to bring it about.

Getting What You Want – and Fulfillment

Ego-driven desires tend not to provide lasting fulfillment, and associated therewith, all forms are transient and impermanent. The key thing is *how we feel* – if we have "gained the world but lost our soul" then fulfillment is missing. But, returning to the subject of materialism, if you really want that new house or new car, or whatever it may be, go ahead and learn from how you feel. It may indeed be a source of pleasure and gratitude for many years to come – and also be of benefit to those close to you. If this is the case, then you have chosen wisely and avoided the trap of "I'll be happy when ..."

Of course, if you are well-off financially, you won't have any difficulty in purchasing things. If, on the other hand, you feel that you have to struggle to get what you want then there is a "cost-benefit" factor to consider. Is the perceived pain (cost) in getting your gain (benefit), going to be worth the price in terms of time, energy, sacrifice and so on?

We can bear in mind that civilization has always progressed, moved onwards and upwards – western civilization was in the midst of the industrial revolution only 200 years go, and just see how things have progressed since then. Our lives are full of conveniences, even if many of these are taken for granted. It seems that no sooner that our conditions improve, we take them for granted as the new norm and we may ask "what's next?!"

If we are truly connected with our Source as forever-Being, (which will tend to keep us purposeful), we will feel joy and as such our needs are already met. Forever-Being is complete and joyful, and the main point about fulfilling desires or destiny is to move towards joy! If we live in the (feeling of) joy as forever-Being, responding to and creating life experiences, what else do we need?

Does this mean that our connection to forever-Being means that we don't have any need for material comforts? Thinking on this, as I sit here writing this book in Thailand, in a classy air-conditioned French restaurant, I realize that my material gains from prior working have been a major source of fulfillment and gratitude. Challenges come up now and again, which I'm normally able to deal with quite rapidly, and so rarely if ever impinge on my wellbeing.

I live very simply in a 5 star apartment near the sea, in glorious weather and a healthy environment. Since my apartment is paid for already, my ongoing accommodation expenses are minimal. While my apartment is quiet and overlooking a national park of religious significance, I have many conveniences within a few minutes walking distance, including reasonably priced 24 hour convenience stores. As I review my life so far, I can feel satisfied that I enjoyed an excellent education, published some articles, had a varied and interesting career, travelled to over 40 countries, and enjoyed so many experiences.

If I hadn't worked and occasionally struggled I would not have the comfort provided by certain *material-benefits* and be able to sit in this relaxed situation to write this book. My life has not been perfect, with some trying relationship issues, yet I have no regrets and appreciate the growth arising from all experiences. We may have to struggle on occasion, yet "this too will pass," nothing is permanent.

So, my personal experience, admittedly ego-driven to a point, suggests that yes, we could all do with arranging our lives in a comfortable and relatively stress-free way that promotes wellbeing. (As we have covered in other Chapters, wellbeing is also connected to our diet, sleep regime, exercise, relationships, habits, environment and connection to forever-Being or Source). Part of this wellbeing can and does arise from *material-benefits* and conveniences so long as healthy choices are made. And, living from ego, glimpses of gratitude arising from certain material benefits, contributes to feeling good. We will not call this joy, because joy is considered to be a feeling without external cause that arises from forever-Being.

Our *destiny*, the subject of this Chapter, and *wellbeing* supported in part by material-benefits, if not synonymous, are highly related. Would we want to forge a destiny that denied our wellbeing? That is not to say that there are not some highly developed spiritual people for whom the externals including *material-benefits* truly have no relevance, and for whom martyrdom for a great and noble cause is an acceptable, perhaps even an enjoyable option.

Never-the-less, while recognizing that some *material-benefits* can support our well-being in an ego-driven world, in this book we are advocating operating from forever-Being. Are you inspired by people that overcome adversity to achieve great things? Or, touched by the poor person who gives away what little he or she has? Is this feeling from the spirit within?

So, what are we advocating here – to be rich or to be poor? If we were cave-men, money would not be necessary, but, here in the 21st Century, money is essential for the basic necessities of life. And while we may not be fans of blatant consumerism and unnecessary consumption, we should want to enjoy at least some of the fruits of advancement. Things like a nice living environment, proximity to conveniences and easy transport which may mean having a nice car. [Of course, some cities are notable by the absence of certain conveniences, heavy traffic, social issues, and pollution, etc. and hopefully we can choose a conducive environment to live].

In order to operate from the state of forever-Being:

1. Live in the present moment, now

2. Know that you are forever-Being, from one Source, connected to Source, living from Source, continuing beyond this human life, yet always, forever, always remaining part of Source

3. Live out of the "JAR" – unstressed from Judgment/ comparison, clingy Attachments/ grasping, Resistance to what is – adopt the attitude "I don't mind what happens" or similar, while ready to make changes if things are not to your liking. Or, you can try to go a stage further to just "love what-is," and know that you are part of the "Oneness" – all that is.

4. You can still visit past and future – still in the now – for example, to retrieve a good memory to be grateful for, to review past experience in order to guide a decision about the future, or to plan the year ahead and so on.

5. You can operate from powerful maxims such as: (i) I don't mind what happens; (ii) I have no problems (in the) Now; (iii) I'm Still Here (Essence) and (iv) I run my own mind (self-mastery)

In order to be fulfilled we need to be living in accordance with our values, which is discussed in the chapters that follow. As we will cover in Chapter 8 on "Love," we need to be in the *flow of life,* and that includes making a *contribution* in ways that feel natural and right to us. This contribution is highly relevant to our destiny or any calling that we feel. And Chapter 10 discusses "Gratitude," an essential practice which provides a cue to focus attention on, and appreciate the abundance already in our lives.

PART 2: Lifestyle Values

CHAPTER 6

The FLAGS Map: Freedom-Love-Adventures-Gratitude-Service

I n the FLAGS Map of personal values to live life by, (shown overleaf), Freedom and Love go together, as do Adventures and Gratitude. The value of Service draws on the other four values.

I have formed and rehashed my personal values, (*beliefs* about what's important personally), many times over the years. Perhaps you have too. Two things that I have found with values is firstly, that they can change over time according to one's life situation or life stage and secondly, knowing one's values takes time in order to get them clear.

Identifying the *right* set of values for you that you can use on a day to day basis is important, as they affect the quality of your life as well, as those around you, and can help you lead a fulfilled life as opposed to one of emptiness or regret, resulting from misguided choices.

Another thing, when you uncover your values, you do not necessarily need to include important things that you have mastered already. If for example you exercise habitually you can exclude "exercise" from your list of values which helps to keep them to a manageable number between 3 and 7. In any event, your health and wellbeing need to be a vitally important part of your lifestyle.

THE FLAGS MAP: FREEDOM AND LOVE TO ADVENTURES AND GRATITUDE AND SERVICE [VALUES]

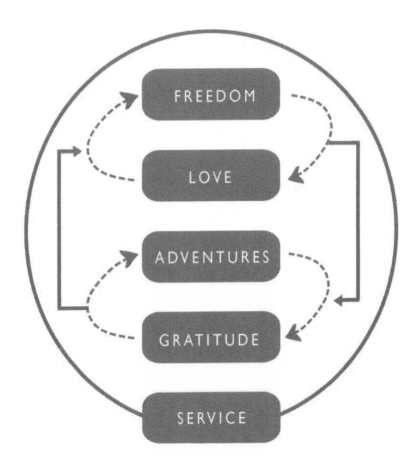

With reference to the FLAGS Map, a sense of *freedom* can be a wonderful free-ing feeling of wellbeing ... an alert, bold (fearless), calm, presence, detached from the concerns of the world, yet ready for anything and fully engaged with the moment. Unburdening from the persona or sense of ego self, allows the flow of life itself, the life-giving creative energy of the universe that can flow through you, out into the world. You express yourself and your unique talents, and make the best of any situation.

This flow of *love* (and courage) leads you into action, adventures, and experiences of life, which in turn can help you to feel gratitude for the good in your life that you have co-created. This might be a hard one for you to swallow just now, but even seemingly negative outcomes may be a source of gratitude as every cloud tends to have a silver lining even if it's difficult to see at the time. Yet if you really trust in life, you will see it more readily, even if only in retrospect. The silver lining could be a lesson learned, a deeper understanding of life, or a change in life direction, and new, more expansive and rewarding experiences. Some seeming misfortunes can turn out to be true blessings.

Probably, it's true you did not ask to be born – I say probably because some people do believe that we had a hand in choosing our life experiences on Earth. In any event, you were created by a force that preceded you and remains part of you, and the day that you were born you inherited the world and more. Your miraculous body works without any conscious effort on your part. As Jesus remarked, the lilies neither toil nor spin, and you don't need to do so either, (unless perhaps you're a Sufi, in which case the latter may apply).

In this FLAGS Map, *adventures* embraces all moments and experiences in every area of your life, the things that make you feel alive, produce happy memories, and help fill your life with gratitude. Things that reflect your voluntary creative self-expression, and add to your joy. Adventures, which often involve overcoming challenges, is what life is all about, as Helen Keller reminds us in her famous quote: "life is an exciting adventure, or nothing at all."

The word *gratitude* might not resonate positively with everyone, because, for example, it might be associated in the mind with its opposite or even worrisome thoughts like "I'm not grateful enough" or "I can't go around saying thank you all the time!" If so, the word *appreciation* might work better for you – the key thing is that gratitude is a *feel-good* feeling, so find words or thoughts that make you feel good about what you have received from life. *The trouble for many of us is that we have been conditioned to have all sorts of needs which are simply unnecessary.* (Typically ones driven by consumerism and that satisfy our ego). Perhaps our biggest need is to "get out of our own way" so that the creative life force can flow through us unimpeded! Perhaps the very things that we take for granted are the things that we should really appreciate the most – think about that one for a minute or two. If you can really feel gratitude for plentiful, yet essential things like air and water then you are on your way. No matter its importance, we have a tendency to discount anything that seemingly, is always there for us, and isn't registering with our ego antenna as harboring a potential problem.

Gratitude and joy are closely interlinked. All renowned and respected spiritual teachers will tell you that loving what-is and not resisting life are key to a full life.

Service is about our attitude towards what we do, as well as giving back, paying forward, contributing, giving, growing and creating - built upon and drawing on the other four Values.

The *five values* embodied in the acronym FLAGS are consistent with living life from the perspective of forever-Being rather than ego. *Freedom* and *love* taken together can be thought of as freeing up the juice for life, while *adventures* and *gratitude* taken together can be thought of as the experience of life itself, a true miracle. In *service*, on the wave of this current human generation, we each play our part in giving back to the whole, each of us fulfilling our purpose as a human being on Planet Earth.

In the chapters that follow, we discuss these five values in more detail.

CHAPTER 7

Freedom

How wonderful to experience a life of true freedom - freedom from anxieties borne out of fear, guilt or worry; freedom to live life on our own terms giving free reign to our talents and aspirations; loving what we do; freedom to choose a lifestyle that provides us with a full life of wellbeing while contributing to the happiness and quality of life for others.

When we feel totally free, we are happy, content, joyous, engaged, one with what we are doing, present, and thriving with no anxieties. We feel good, are in the flow, connected to our divinity, and not resisting or arguing with anything in our current reality. We love everyone and everything, and potentially petty woes and concerns, our resistances to the flow of love, die to naught.

The starting point for the various freedoms outlined above is psychological freedom, an element of mind-set. The biggest obstacles to feeling free that we will ever face are of the mind and body, which is to say our thoughts and emotions, and our moods. With the right **mind**-set, (conscious, creative), and **mood**, (poise, bold-calm), one can learn to be happy no matter what, and to change things where necessary, for example, if faced with an untoward social, work, home, or general living environment. Happiness only requires a few basic conditions, and the *decision* to be free, happy and blissful. So to experience freedom, we must work on getting the right mind-set and mood, while engaging with life in a way that is purposeful and meaningful.

Freedom, requires that we get ourselves to a point where we are living life on our own terms, largely through *attention management*, thereby maintaining a good mood and living consciously, to create a life of love and meaning, lived from the heart. A good mood is essential to freedom because you cannot be free if absorbed, possessed or imprisoned by a bad mood.

How do we maintain a good mood? Through our mind-body and senses. Each human knows their world through the *perceptions* of the conventionally accepted five senses, (sight, sound, smell, taste, touch), and mind-body (thoughts-emotions and feelings). In our day to day concerns, we too often forget to pay attention to making good use of our senses and mind-body choices. Your mood is influenced by the *choices* that you make in three areas:

1. Environments   **[Place]** (Scenery, sound, safety, facilities, air quality, climate, culture, regulation, cleanliness, economy, etc.); home, work, social
2. Relationships   **[People]** Ego self, others. And, **True Self**
3. Body-mind   [**Physiology, Positive Psychology**]

    Sleep, diet, exercise, rest and rejuvenation; meditation, hypnosis, etc.

These three aspects are mutually dependent. If you have a good relationship with yourself, for example, you are more likely to take care of your body, and optimize your environments. Your personal values will help you to make aligned, conscious choices.

From the vantage of personal freedom, we will want to perform unselfish, inspired actions for others, even for our Planet, out of pure love and compassion for humanity and for all-life. Ironically, then, freedom, a casting off of external or internal oppressions, a removal of our chains, involves recognizing our Oneness and giving to the Whole, which is ultimately the One-self of which we are part. (If you want to understand evidence of Oneness more, please refer to the Introduction).

Another way to look at freedom is to be free of afflictions:

1. Mental afflictions – negativity such as fear, guilt, apathy, sadness
2. Bodily afflictions – impacting health, comfort, mobility, energy
3. Soul afflictions – feeling separation, isolation, cut off from Source or benevolent universe

Again, if you pay close *attention* to managing your *mind* and *mood*, you will be shielded from these afflictions. More accurately, these afflictions will become irrelevant to as you choose to focus your attention away from "monkey-mind" to the good in your life.

There are people in this world with very severe physical disabilities, yet some are happy because they are not burdened by a false sense of self, and are able to accept their situation with equanimity. In effect, freedom arises from our "State," living in the present moment, and seeing or sensing through the "Eyes of forever-Being," surrendered to, and loving, what-is.

Quoting Byron Katie:
"No one can give you freedom but you ... the only time we suffer is when we believe a thought that argues with what is. When the mind is perfectly clear, what-is, is what we want."

This is consistent with spiritual teachers who advise people to say or think "I don't mind what happens," and further to accept things as if they had chosen them. Yet Katie came up with the above statement in quotes, and other linking ideas, independently, and based on her painful personal experiences. Her book "Loving What Is," and her four question methodology for questioning beliefs that she calls "The Work," and mentioned earlier, are well worth following up.

A simple definition of freedom is to live in total presence, surrendered to, and at one with reality. Take note! Living from presence and mindfulness, all the other elements of a fulfilling life fall into place as we gain the right insights and make wise life-choices.

A life of true freedom and peace requires that we understand who we are and operate from our *forever-Being* rather than "ego", the ultimately, fear-based, thoughts and stories in our heads. *Forever-Being* is synonymous with living in the present moment, oneness with "what-is," reality, the flow of expansive love-energy and joy, while ego is synonymous with past and future, separation, delusion, constriction and pain.

Operating from *forever-Being* in the moment, we are free to follow a joyous path. We develop effective beliefs, knowing and behaviors, accepting the rightness of our choices with fruitful results for ourselves and others. We accept any unconsciousness on our part, as a process to learn life's lessons, and to make course corrections.

Forever-Being = Loving what-is (God's creations, reality) = Loving God/ Source, etc. = Freedom. Freedom is appreciating everything in a state of awareness, free of attachments and aversions, or any other mental afflictions.

Some Obstacles to Freedom

Obstacles to freedom include:

Judgment: A small tree isn't inferior to a larger tree, so it is with all of nature, things are as they are. That's it. And, things are as they are according to the particular environment and seeds or intentions present. While it may be difficult not to judge people and situations against your values, standards, and desire for a happier world; you need to accept that which you cannot change, and realize that people are acting from their present level of consciousness and conditioning in making any unwise choices.

Attachments: Attachments have a hold over you, and can therefore cause you emotional pain if their existence is threatened. In true freedom we are free of our attachments. We can never be free if we really need and cling to something – what we want to possess, possesses us!! And in possessing us, it can tease, terrify and frustrate us with feelings like disappointment or resentment.

Our attachments can include:

- "Comfort zone" discussed towards the end of this chapter.
- Addictions to drama in relationships, our ailments, sex, food, drugs, etc.
- Mind-chatter (see "Rumination" below), likes and dislikes, and limiting beliefs
- "Needs" identified by Maslow, McClelland, Herzberg and other psychologists such as physiological (sex, sleep, food), security (money, property, etc.), belonging, social affiliation and approval, power or control, achievement; recognition and fame, self-actualization.

"Moderation in all things" is a good adage to live by, although that expression isn't necessarily to act as a curb on healthy desires. The best thing is to have and enjoy things without needing them or causing unnecessary waste. Materialism is discussed in more detail in Chapter 9: "Adventures."

Resistance: As the old saying goes "what you resist persists." The time-based ego is a bit like a "resistor" in an electrical circuit, and may be subject to overheating.

These three key obstacles can be remembered by the acronym JAR, and the word "jar" may be thought of as a container of these undesirable, potentially painful elements, or mind "baggage."

Rumination on painful thoughts about what has happened, or will happen, would cause you to suffer. (Rumination can be regarded as part of the "attachment" categorization above, through identification with your story, for example). If you have concerns about the future, taking pre-emptive action based on clear thought and assessment in the present, may be the most appropriate course, and might involve enlisting external support if necessary. The past has gone and if the memories are unhappy ones, then you can just observe the temporary associated emotions and choose to let them go. You might consider reframing them, and if they are persistent, obtaining professional help. You need to look for the lesson, changes, actions or avoidance strategies for the future, and the associated blessings too. And, don't forget to give self- acceptance.

In what I jokingly refer to as Tolle's let out clause, you can be free to follow your preferences in many "non-acceptable" situations. (In one video clip, Eckhart Tolle gives the example of when he moved to a different seat on a bus to avoid proximity to certain individuals liable to challenge his peace).

Environmental toxicity: This can refer to social, political, economic, physical, climatic, cultural, work-place and family conditions. Hopefully you live and contribute your gifts in a country and place where you can feel safe and supported and experience growth. If not, you need to find a solution to your situation while developing your inner strength and coping skills. You may need to walk away from a situation, however painful, consistent with your values and vision, yet consider the impact on others, especially innocent people, and act responsibly. This may be a difficult call.

Some Enablers of Freedom

In practical terms, as we go through life, we find ourselves dealing with people and situations.

In dealing with *situations* and events that are not to our liking, we can adopt a "**LUCKY**" attitude. This is an acronym to remind us to firstly, (and primarily),

to have gratitude for how lucky we are, and then to come into situations from a perspective of **L**ove, **U**nderstanding, **C**ompassion, **K**indness and Jo**Y**. Gratitude

for what we have, have had or will have, is really important when confronting difficult situations where we sense loss. And, whatever is happening right now, why not remind yourself that great things are about to happen.

When *people* issues come up, we may need to practice, **F**orgiveness, **A**cceptance, **C**almness, **E**mpathy and **S**upport to wellbeing and happiness, which can be remembered by the acronym **FACES**. This doesn't mean that you have to agree

with people all the time if you see things differently but you can at least try to understand the other's perspective. Instead of automatically resisting and rejecting another's idea for example, try to find a way to accommodate it. You might come across a more acceptable idea that builds on the intentions of the one presented to you. Or you might acknowledge "you may be right," unless you're absolutely sure of your facts.

The acronyms LUCKY and FACES can be applied to yourself too. As within, so without. You show up according to how you feel about yourself. The more secure you feel within yourself, the less threatening life situations will be.

In dealing with both people and situations we can operate from a positive stance embodied in the acronym **SCHOOL: S**miling, **C**onfident, **H**appy, double **O**ptimistic, **L**over of Life.

So there you have it: LUCKY FACES SCHOOL.

The Art of Surrender

Surrender is like Sunshine to the Soul.
"Whatever you accept you go beyond – that's a miracle. If you fight it you're stuck with it!" The perfect state is the acceptance of now. (And), *surrender opens up the vertical dimension.* Eckhart Tolle

Don't let anything – thought, feeling idea, concept or anything else, stick to, ensnare or grab you. Living in the Now in a state of Surrender is the answer.

If you let go a little, you will have a little peace. If you let go a lot, you will have a lot of peace. If you let go completely, you will know complete peace and freedom. Your struggles with the world will have come to an end. Ajahn Chah, (also known as the Thai forest monk).

Allowing everything to be *as it is* frees you from a lot of negativity. Suffering = pain x resistance, so the more you resist, the more you suffer. Consistent with this equation, the Buddha likened "pain" to a first arrow piercing the flesh and "resistance" as the second arrow. Colloquially, we may say "don't rub it in" or remind us.

Resistance is synonymous with ego and causes suffering. If resistance (of the mind) is zero, then there is no suffering. We may feel discomforting emotion: if so, just observe and accept it, as it's only a feeling. Focusing on the breath will also help take your mind off it and the impermanent emotion will die away. If change is called for, put things in motion from a place of presence and calmness.

Surrender goes way beyond acceptance. It applies to everything covered under "Obstacles to Freedom" above. In surrender there is no negativity – whatever the cause – attachment, judgment and comparison, resisting the present situation or anything else. Nirvana is dropping everything. Surrender is the ultimate dropping tool. In surrender, you do and enjoy things, but you don't get lost in, addicted to, or fret over outcomes.

Time Freedom

One of the main misconceptions about living in the present moment is that there is to be no time allotted for reflection, planning ahead and goal setting. This is not the case and Eckhart Tolle writing in The Power of Now, neatly distinguishes between what he calls clock time and psychological time. Essentially clock time refers to productive time that may be used in reflection or planning ahead for example. This is conscious, potentially highly creative time. This time element also corresponds with the "not urgent, important" quality time quadrant of the urgency/ importance matrix introduced by the late Steven Covey, (author of the 7 Habits of Highly Productive People), among others.

So you can be calm, present, and be a "go-giver," contributing your gifts to the world.

Psychological time refers to time spent on things that are potentially stressing such as the worry habit of ruminating on painful past events, or anxieties about future events. Now, we can't go burying our heads in the sand all the time, and life will send us some curve-balls from time to time that we may have to prepare for and deal with.

Developing habits of surrender and acceptance, and understanding the ways of nature and impermanence, can help us to deal with everything much more easily. Our waking time can be divided as follows:

Fully in the Now Time (NT) + Clock Time (CT) + Psychological Time (PT) = 100%.

Ideally perhaps, on average, NT=80%, CT=20% and PT=0% and this will vary from day to day. Despite the distinctions it is always "Now."

One needs to be careful, that clock time doesn't descend, or drift, into psychological time. Psychological Time is synonymous with resistance of the ego.

As human beings, we have a tendency to act from a sense of separation with Source, argue with the reality of what-is, ruminate, have clingy attachments, and often have a certain level of background anxiety about this or that, according to our life situation. In order to counter these tendencies, and to experience more joy, fulfillment and happiness, a shift needs to take place as illustrated in the SHIFT Map overleaf.

In essence, we need to operate from Loving **P**resence, **O**neness, **S**urrender and **E**nough (or completeness). [This can be remembered by the acronym contained in "Loving POSE"].

In the SHIFT Map, the shift may be whole, as in flipping a switch or may be graduated between 0 and 100%. The abbreviations on the map are as follows: L-Loving, F-Fearful, P-Present/Peaceful, D-Disturbed, ONE-Oneness, SEP-Separateness, S-Surrendered, R-Resistant, E-Enough (or Complete), N-Needy.

You may contrast this Map with the AAAA Map in Chapter 2, which is not competing, but provides a complementary model that helps drive home the spiritual principles underpinning awakening, wellbeing and purposeful achievement.

THE SHIFT MAP: Separateness to Oneness
From Time Dependence, trapped in ego, characterized by:

- Autopilot
- Horizontal dimension (past/ future)
- Conditioned unconsciousness
- Resistance, mind energy

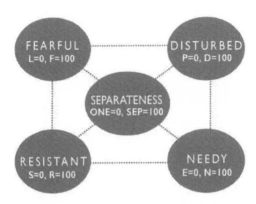

To Time Freedom, living as forever-Being characterized by:

- Deliberate living
- Vertical dimension (now)
- Non-conditioned consciousness
- Flow, essence energy

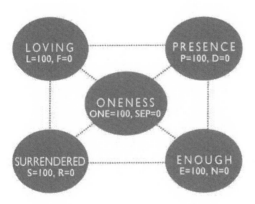

In the Shift Map there are 5 variables, and the shift is (1) from being *fearful* to being *loving*, (2) from *disturbed* (mind) to being *present*, (3) from *separateness* (ego sense of self) to *oneness* (with Being), (4) from *resistant* (mind) to surrendered; and finally (5) a shift from being *needy* and sensing lack, to feeling *enough*, grateful and abundant in our attitude to life.

In practice you may recognize yourself on either side of the shift, depending on whether your *life situation* feels positive (encouraging), neutral (comfortable), or negative (challenging).

In general, when identifying top priorities it is sometimes possible to find a key one that has the maximum impact on all key aspects being considered. There is a reference to finding the "one thing" in the Bible, and in a book entitled "The One Thing" by Gary Keller with Jay Papasan, the one thing is found in answer to the question: "What is the one thing I can do such that by doing it, everything else will become easier or unnecessary?" The "One Thing" in the Shift Map is Oneness with forever-Being and "all-that-is."

Oneness: If we can really sense and feel this Oneness with forever-Being and life itself, we will have entered the timeless vertical dimension of now, will be in the flow or zone, feel abundant and have a loving or benign disposition.

How do we get it then? Well, first it's important to focus your awareness on awareness. Attention on the other 4 variables in the "Shift Map" will certainly help and they are elaborated upon in the sub-sections following this one. Knowledge and understanding helps. Consider for example:

- Life is a continuum of constant flux and change; life and death are merely transitions in the life continuum, and death of a temporary form is not to be feared. All forms are impermanent.
- *Atomically* we and our universe are more than 99.9999% space so we are more space than anything else in common with the rest of the universe. Can you know yourself as the space?

- A strong faith, a knowing, a clear perception that there is an infinite intelligence out of which we are all born – the Tao, space, stillness, silence, formlessness, ….
- A realization that it's our strong sense of self and separateness that gets us into so much trouble and drama!
- A realization that paradoxically we don't matter at all and will be quite quickly forgotten, yet we are also potentially incredibly important in this brief temporary form
- We are the current expression of creation at the forefront of time with only future ahead; there is nothing that we have to do, yet we will want to contribute to life

Loving is all about exuding a benign positive energy out into the world, and devoid of any anxiety or fear, because you are not burdened with a sense of a poor, separate, vulnerable self to protect and defend at every turn. You will know the wisdom of kindness, and have compassion for the struggles of others who are living from separation and lack, and suffering emotionally. Note that the way that you treat yourself is a cue for how you treat others, so let yourself off the hook and love yourself first, as a pre-requisite for loving others. Let go of the past and create the future out of the now. Live in warm appreciation of all that life has to offer.

Presence is all about taking energy or attention away from your mind's preoccupation with past and future, typically by focusing on an anchor such as your breath or inner energy field. And, while being fully alert and aware of reality: observing the wonders and beauty of life in its perfection, even when it seems imperfect. In meditation, you focus your attention on a particular object, gently concentrating your awareness. In mindfulness your attention is non-judgmental and concerned with whatever you are doing in the moment.

Surrender is all about letting go of resistance and attachments of the mind in response to our life situation moment to moment. It is surrendering to the life energy, the love energy of the Creator. In common with the "Enough" variable, know that all you really need is a roof over your head, some shelter, food and exercise. Therein lies sufficient safety for your ego. Trust that in getting out of your own way and being relieved of the burden of a separate self, you will naturally feel "uncaused" joy.

Enough is all about recognizing deeply that you are already enough and complete, and this is closely related to self-acceptance. This sense of being enough and complete is important, because virtually 100% of people grow up believing that they are somehow lacking – and this is true from ego-perspective. As a child, you may have learned to associate love with accomplishment, for example, because any praise you received from adults was conditional upon performing things they considered important. You may have been compared unfavorably with siblings or others, or, having picked up society's rules you did the comparing, and judged yourself less or more capable than others. Of course, at any stage of your life you may sense a need to become competent in an area of your choosing, yet you remain enough at all times.

In Chapter 1, we provided a brief question and answer session with a tree. If we look at nature, we can see that there is no need to be judgmental about the characteristics of different life forms. We can see that a tree started as a seed, (such as an acorn that produces an oak tree), with certain potentialities for showing-up in the world. Trees grow up according to the nature of the earth, climate etc., which is to say its environment. It had no choice and could not be otherwise. Like you, the tree seemingly did not ask to be born, it just is. It is fully enough just as it was created according to its blueprint (or seed) and environment, and of course, the same applies to you.

The big difference between you and a tree is your ability to choose, and we are assuming free-will, yet even that may be questionable, since your responses to the external environment, (choices and decisions), have been commensurate with your seeds of potentiality that you had at, or prior to, the moment of your birth.

Refer also to the end of this chapter for a list of practices consistent with the SHIFT Map.

Enlightenment

Related to the Shift Map above, enlightenment is living in the light of aware-ness, in the present moment, in a State of Being beyond the ordinary mind, which is simply to say, unaffected by passing unconscious thoughts and emo-tions; in Eckhart Tolle's words, your natural state of felt Oneness with Being, (at the core of the SHIFT Map), ... your true nature beyond name and form. The Buddha defines enlightenment very simply as the end of suffering.

If you are enlightened, you have awakened to your heart, to the light, to your connection with Source. Enlightenment gives you the power to bring light to darkness in the present moment, relinquishing attachment to past and future, and saying yes to "what-is."

In surrender, there is no mind resistance, which effectively means that this is the end of the ego-mind as master. This is a state of grace and lightness, a state without struggle. Pain can be felt and observed without making a story out of it, thereby causing pain to lose power and dissolve.

Enlightened people "don't mind what happens," and are free from the psycho-logical suffering that can emanate from unconscious reactive mind patterns, or thoughts and emotions connected with potentially disturbing situations, people and physical pain. Enlightened people accept their completeness, (already fully "enough" as forever-Being), sense the abundance of the universe/ life force, and do not feel the need to cling emotionally, thereby avoiding pain or suffering.

Spiritual masters advise that enlightenment cannot be a goal, because it can only be our experience this very (present) moment. Making enlightenment into a goal is to ensure that it will always be in the future and therefore elusive. Yet at some later now, enlightenment may happen to you, and this could be as a result of disciplined inner work or, in comparatively rare cases, can be a spon-taneous, natural reaction to severe emotional turmoil, (as discussed a couple of paragraphs below). You will know if you are truly enlightened by the joy and peace that you feel, and your acceptance of all that is without stress You would experience no fear of so-called "death," and an absence of worry about things, that hitherto, would have made you feel anxious. Yet being enlightened doesn't make you into a god, albeit you would be identified with true self, the formless, timeless, invisible life force or essence. You would not be totally immune to the death of loved ones, yet you would bring in acceptance a lot more readily than hitherto and feel at peace. Knowing that nature's cycle is continuing as normal, and that their essence has just moved on to the next of life's mysteries, would help lessen your time spent in grief.

Rather than making enlightenment a goal, what you can do is make *freedom* both a value and a goal. We are talking of freedom here as transcendence of, the ego-mind of past and future, and living in a state of presence and relaxed surrender, of non-resistance to what is. Basically, nothing bothers you, yet you will help to bring about change where you feel it is necessary. This is more than a dogged determination not to be fazed by anything, *it's more a realization that there is nothing to be bothered about.* Nothing bothers you, even if you recognize the need for it to change. And, with your inner change, the outer world will change to. You need to observe the ego, both thoughts and emotions. Unconscious thoughts arising are only for your consideration, and subject to your conscious modification. Painful emotions once observed, tend to dissolve as mentioned earlier.

It is generally recognized that people will avoid change until they have really had enough. Indeed, Eckhart Tolle and Byron Katie are two well-known people that went through the hell of being possessed by their own minds; this got to a point that a sudden radical change or conversion came over them, opening them to a new consciousness or awareness, where they were no longer attached to, and identified with, their painful unconscious thoughts and emotions. It could be said that they transcended their ego. Unless you have a transformative experience that leads to instant enlightenment, you will have to accept that it would take a lot of practice and time before you tip the scales so to speak, and sense the enlightenment that you are. We need to question and break free of old conditioning that doesn't serve us, and be conscious creators in the here and now. And, rooted in the knowledge that through evolution, you are both God's child (form), and essence (formless). Realizing the need to not-resist life, surrender is key to allowing the vibration of joy to be felt within your body. This is the "kingdom of heaven within" that surpasses the pursuit of pleasure alone.

On the journey from ego to forever-Being, from conditioned unconsciousness to non-conditioned consciousness, I believe that you are only as enlightened as you can be this moment. Some people have had glimpses of enlightenment and it is rare for anyone to remain perpetually in the enlightened state. Our state of consciousness, and propensity for enlightenment varies with our **mood** and **mind** in each moment.

Moving from the Prison of Victimhood to the Freedom of Presence

We can recognize four stages in opening to awareness and true freedom:

1. Victimhood: slave to ego thoughts and emotions, stories, limiting beliefs,
2. Empowered: realization of self-responsibility for results; examined and changed beliefs
3. Acceptance: seeing the light and learning to go with the Creator's flow
4. Awareness: self-mastery and cognizance of true self; effective attention and energy management

The **Victimhood Mode** is characterized by blame, fault finding, complaining and denying responsibility. The victim is locked in his or her "ego cocoon." When things go wrong it's always someone else's fault, and there is an unwillingness to see how one may have contributed in some way or circumvented the situation. Unwise choices, and unrealistic expectations, beliefs or assumptions, are examples of how people can sabotage their happiness and feel like victims.

The **Empowered Mode** is characterized by a realization of one's own power, for example, as expressed in "if it's going to be it's up to me" and a solution-oriented approach to manifesting results. This is the mode or stage that most conventionally successful people are in. If you were lucky, your upbringing would have conditioned you for this mode, (rather than victimhood), although there may have been some elements of victimhood that crept in too.

Even so, excessive domination of this mode without spiritual connection, can lead to a lack of fulfillment, as referred to earlier in this book. In the extreme this could amount to "gaining the world and losing one's soul," as one religious text suggests.

The **Acceptance Mode** already alluded to in the "AAAA Map," (Chapter 2 refers), is characterized by an understanding that there is no such thing as "I'll be happy when," having discovered first-hand the impermanence of things, people, situations and painful or pleasurable emotions. There is a greater worldly "knowingness" that eventually, all things turn into rust and dust. In acceptance, the resistance of fearful EGO, (edging god out), is gradually giving way to Surrendering to the Sunshine of Source and the creative energy of our Creator.

Unless exposed to spirituality early on in life, it's comparatively rare for people to live in acceptance and surrender, (if at all), until they are well into middle-age. By this time, many people have experienced the "outward movement" as Tolle puts it, typically having built a family, career and a nest-egg that can be used in any retirement. This is followed by experiencing the "inward movement," as people having experienced the ups and downs of life, now have more security and time for reflection.

In the acceptance mode there is a loving acceptance of what-is, a greater sense of inter-connectedness, the recognition that like begets like, and a growing desire to be kind. The saying "I don't mind what happens" is no longer just an aphorism but becoming a reality in one's life. As the British rock group Queen sing in their song Bohemian Rhapsody, "Nothing really matters to me." You have begun to awaken. Living a simple life without unnecessary drama, and experiencing more time in meditation and stillness is helpful. At the same time, there is no reason not to be fully engaged with life according to your capacity and wellbeing.

The **Awareness Mode** is characterized by a calm mind, an absence of "baggage," and greater clarity of reality by virtue of being fully immersed in the here and now. Having experienced the empowered and acceptance modes, the aware person has learned to process his or her emotions and beliefs, and lives in a more or less permanent state of peace, love, joy and gratitude. In the world but not of it, the aware person is relatively untroubled by personal or worldly woes while keen to make a positive difference and contribution.

It is possible to live temporarily in higher states or modes, and then slip back into lower states, especially if feeling unwell or sleep-deprived, for example, which lowers your mood and state of wellbeing. People living in the empowered mode can at times fall back into the victimhood mode of complaining. In a similar way that meditation practitioners have to constantly remind themselves to re-focus on their object of attention, (typically, but not always, the breath), higher state aspirers need to remind themselves to return to the higher state. And, this may first require attention to factors underlying a bad mood. It may help to study or listen to the words of great *life coaches* that may resonate with you. These life-coaches may include Buddha, Jesus, Krishna; more contemporary spiritual teachers such as Tolle, Mooji, and Adyashanti; and, more moderately, life coaches such as Anthony (Tony) Robbins, Jack Canfield, Robin Sharma and Brian Tracy. Just be careful that where abundance and becoming rich are discussed, that the emphasis is on wellbeing and doing what you love, or at least of being of service and contributing, rather than purely money-motivated.

It seems that many people do not get much beyond the victimhood state with occasional success in the empowered state. Most people have to work on themselves very diligently to spend significant time in the acceptance and awareness modes. Your wellbeing and positive impact on the world will definitely increase considerably if you do the inner work required.

In the case of dedicated Buddhists and others concerned about karma and the next life, making the transition through the 4 stages or modes is particularly important. As discussed under "Enlightenment," a very small number of people, who typically go on to become spiritual teachers, have a spontaneous switch from victimhood/ empowered states to awareness, with the primary characteristic being freedom from entertaining painful thoughts; they became able to drop the baggage of the past, and accept what-is.

The characteristics of this switch, seem to embody Love, Presence, Oneness, Surrender, and feeling "Enough" as discussed under "Time Freedom" earlier in this chapter. So fed up were these people with their painful states that they somehow determined not to be captivated by these negative states ever-ever again. An absolute and seemingly permanent refusal to get caught up! A bit like "been there, done that" – never again! Enough is enough!! *If only, we could all reach this perspective that suffering is unnecessary, a simple choice. Can you get it?* It may be simply a case of fierce resolution, or simply realizing the futility and insanity of allowing oneself to get caught up in the ego's nonsense, or you may have to delve into and change the beliefs that underpin difficult emotions.

There is a need to both transform and detach from the conditioning out of which our thoughts and feelings arise. We read stories of people who have been on the spiritual path for decades who haven't progressed very far. This may be because they cannot sufficiently transform their baggage or detach from it. The ability to detach from all that is not you, and live in acceptance of the now is crucial.

Bear in mind too that *Suffering = Pain x Resistance*, so if there is no resistance, there is no suffering either. This reinforces the wisdom of "acceptance." Refuse to get upset and deal with things calmly at a suitable time. If there's a task ahead that you don't relish - completing your tax return perhaps – just do it and avoid thinking about it, except maybe to contemplate the benefits of task completion that might include a reward that you have promised yourself.

Perhaps our mind's seeming struggle through these four modes or states is analogous to the metamorphosis of a caterpillar to a butterfly, and perhaps humans are indeed in the early stage of an evolutionary "flowering of consciousness."

Awareness and Enlightenment

This book provides a variety of different Maps, along with a certain amount of deliberate repetition, in order to look at enlightenment and awareness in different ways, some of which may resonate with you more than others.

With reference to the ABCDE Map below, **Awareness** is synonymous with **Detachment**, a letting go of all things false, and full acceptance of what-is. (Note that non-attachment or detachment is at the core of Buddha teachings). The inner quality of awareness allows us to sense the **Beauty** of life in our world, and to give **Compassion** and facilitate change where unconsciousness is found. Living in awareness, we are One-with-Life, "Surrendered to the Sunshine of Source," fearless, and seeing through the "Eyes of Being," the heart.

THE ABCDE MAP: ENLIGHTENMENT

Awareness	Beauty
Enlightenment	
Detachment	Compassion

In *awareness and detachment*, our internal environment, there is peace from mind, and a fearless reverence for life. Being "in the world but not of it," and to "deny thyself" – as Jesus put it, makes us problem and worry free. Freed from the burden of ego-self, moments of bliss may arise, the uncaused energy of joy from our Creator/ Source as we get out of our own way and sense the beauty and miracles all around us. Referring back to Dr. Hawkins vibrational power scale, if living from high vibration, one would see with *compassion* many people, (who did not ask to be born), struggling and stuck in their conditioning at lower vibrational levels. This provides an immense opportunity for those living in a higher orbit, to help raise consciousness and help others achieve freedom.

Becoming Fearless

Oh, to be free of fear is a great feeling – a place inside where nothing can faze you or make you feel constricted, small or incomplete. Fear prevents you from *appreciating* – be it appreciation in the sense of personal *growth* or of *gratitude*. It constricts your awareness and ties you to fearful thoughts and emotions. It makes you feel resistant to what-is. It takes you out of accepting the present moment.

Some authorities say that all fear is ultimately related to the fear of death. Let's assume for the time being that this is true, and so let's look at the two alternative scenarios present at our death.

When we die there appear to be two options:
(a) We move on to a new adventure, perhaps like a caterpillar metamorphosing into a butterfly, (albeit our formless Being first merging, reuniting or remaining with the life force of consciousness; as a side note, Buddhists generally believe we move back to form according to our karma).
(b) We have no further experiences or *awareness* after our human "death"

If (a) applies then no worries, look forward both to enjoying life - and your pending after-death adventure! If (b) applies, then how daft we are to take our lives so seriously! Choose joy while you can!!

Of course, we have already argued in the Introduction that you are *forever-Being* and so only (a) applies. Unfortunately, with option (a) the main religions contain an element of the possibility of *hell and brimstone*, including Buddhism perhaps surprisingly, in that Buddhists believe that after death, one could return as an animal and be severely held back in the aim of achieving enlightenment in a future lifetime; bad karma can hamper progress.

We do not subscribe to the possibility of a future hell and brimstone, only that life on Earth is a mirror of our inner state, and that the hell or heaven we experience is self-created in our own minds in reaction to situations or events. Still, if you're unsure about it, best to err on the side of the angels in your thoughts, emotions and especially behaviors! The fact is, if we truly act from the belief in *forever-Being* and *Oneness* we cannot but be kind and compassionate and reap the rewards of our behavior. Moreover if we have erred, sinned, missed the mark in the past due to our unconsciousness, we have to forgive our unconsciousness and move on – onwards and upwards! (Recall the acronym FACES).

There is logic in the Buddhist notion, (and core Buddhism is regarded as a philosophy by some rather than a religion), that our karma impacts us post-death because death is only a shedding of our present human form in the everlasting and continuous movement of life. (So there is no need to differentiate between pre-death and post death in terms of the continuum of all life and our own consciousness). As a note of accuracy, while re-birth is part of Buddhism, in actual fact, notions of re-birth pre-date the Buddhism into which it was incorporated.

Getting back to what fear is all about, beyond death, (which may be an umbrella fear), fears can be categorized as (a) rational or real, (such as the man-eating tiger in the room!); (b) irrational or unreal, (typically imaginary scary stories or fantasies that we tell ourselves that rarely come to pass); and (c) what might be called reasonable fears, (related to anticipated hardships that can reasonably be foreseen and, so indeed, will quite plausibly arise from new choices, realities or situations).

Many day to day fears tend to stem from our perception of **needs** to survive and thrive, with feelings related to safety, comfort, acceptance and appreciation being particularly important. Fears generally revolve around the following:
1. Fear of loss (or diminishment of what you are, possess or enjoy)
2. Fear of not enough (of what you desire for your future)

These fears can lead to the quest for more, more, more! While this is definitely alright up to a point, eventually this may be accompanied by limited fulfillment and diminishing returns on our level of happiness. And, unless you're doing what you love for the best part, the question arises as to whether or not the perceived gain is worth the perceived pain.

We can feel stuck as we face difficult or conflicting choices as to our best course of action. Then again, some reframing and reprogramming (or reconditioning) of our mind with more empowering beliefs would put a different perspective on the situation.

Below we elaborate further on fears of "loss" or "not enough."

Fear Category	Things that we may Fear (or feel concerned about)
Fear of loss or diminishment	*Physical:* injury; disease, treatment, discomfort, loss of sense faculties; death *Material:* loss of money, possessions, conveniences, etc. *Mental:* loss of mental faculties such as memory, etc. *Obligations:* unwanted tasks, situations or expectations *Phobias:* insects, open spaces, etc. *Emotional:* loss of love, acceptance, popularity, status *Behavioral:* inability to cope or perform; making decisions; trusting life and people
Fear of not enough	Not enough time, talent, qualifications, strength, money, attractiveness, love, acceptance, approval, adventure, good things, confidence, worth, motivation, energy, ambition, , experience, recognition, respect, capacity, happiness, joy, etc.

Some common examples of fears include:
- Not being good enough – e.g. lacking competence, inferiority issues
- Not being loved enough or rejected – e.g. fear that family members do not love or approve of you, fear that your spouse may leave you, or fear of being alone or without a real soul-mate
- Not having enough – e.g. maybe I'll become destitute and end up on the streets – and my family will look down on me!! (He/ she didn't "make-it").

- Lack of control over our lives – the feeling of being stuck in a rut, not knowing how to get out easily
- Lack of trust in someone or something – e.g. uncertainty that someone will deliver the goods; or concerns about making the right choices for your future; procrastination
- Bondage or unwanted obligations that detract from your joy – e.g. an unfulfilling job with little opportunity to improve the job situation or your perception of it
- Inability to find fulfillment in the future – can include rapid-risers and the wealthy who already "have it all" – what's left or what's next?!

We are always enough, the way that we were created. As human beings we have free will and choice, yet imperfect knowledge and so have to learn how to do our best in an uncertain world. This is our predicament and our adventure. We have to live from love, not fear.

The impact of fear is to stress and constrict us emotionally. We are each one entity within the whole, and our mind and body are intimately interconnected. Mental stress, dis-ease, can cause disease in our bodies. This is not to say that all stress is to be avoided and a term *eustress* has been coined to identify healthy levels of stress that can both drive and fulfil us. Not everyone experiences stress in the same way though – what is a very big deal to some people is "water off a duck's back" or relatively trivial for others.

Sometimes the subject of fear is introduced by reference to saber-toothed tigers, or other primordial conditions, which is fine if the development of the human brain forms part of the discussion. Yet, even in this modern age, we are born into the world in vulnerable conditions. As pointed out before, just one false step in crossing the road and kaput! (This is more readily observable in cities of the developing world, where one needs eyes not only at the back of one's head, but to the side as well). Lives are more complicated now than back in the stone-age, for example, in the number of roles people play, albeit we are compensated with a lot more comfortable modern facilities courtesy of our ancestors.

What then, are the antidotes to fear? Note that our fears fall into two related categories – loss or not enough – so if we really **know** and feel that, we have **nothing to lose** (or resist), and that we are **already enough,** we can be fearless. *If we can "let go" completely, and have no-needs or sense of lack, we can be fearless.*

Indeed, letting go and surrendering is perhaps the most powerful antidote to fear. Paradoxically, in this state one doesn't mind what happens at all, while at the same time has a deep reverence for all. How awesome is that? Surrendering to the moment, one can maintain a calm and bold mood expressed from forever-Being rather than from ego. Further, there is an irony in that when we don't hold on and crave something, it can sometimes find its way to us more easily.

A useful phrase or mantra to recall if facing loss or lack is, "I Am Still Here" or "I Am Still, Here," recognizing that whatever thoughts and emotions you are experiencing, your *essence* has not changed at all. This can be a cue for you to enter the State of Surrender – relaxed, calm, loving what-is.

Surrendering means total acceptance and oneness with the situation, allowing things to be as they are, and getting out of our own way. In this state we can instigate purposeful change from the perspective of forever-Being. And, in this way, we are not a slave to the trance of fearful thoughts, and consequent reactions, that may not serve us or others well.

More than anything else, it's our thoughts that cause us to be happy or suffer. **Learn to feel safe, still and serene** and thereby become unstoppable, confident and a joy to yourself and others.

Comfort Zone

To be or not to be in our *Comfort Zone*... that is the question? I think that we do need to get out of our comfort zone sometimes, though I would not necessarily advocate making oneself "scared every day" as some life coaches suggest. Approached the right way though, it could really be quite exciting to be making regular breakthroughs through challenging fears.

Yet, infinitely better than getting out of your comfort zone, is for you to actually *expand* your comfort zone, so that you feel comfortable growing through bigger challenges for the benefit of yourself and others, without undue stress. Part of the purpose of this book has been to help you expand your view of what's possible without scaring yourself to death! Indeed, we advocate authentic, fearless living as far as practicable, doing what's right for you. Enlisting a good coach to help you reprogram your beliefs, and to stay accountable to your goals and dreams, is a great way to expand your comfort zone and achieve success.

Living as forever-Being in cohorts with the permanent Oneness, is arguably the best antidote for combatting fear. There is safety in trusting the permanent! Even the best and most well-intentioned people may let us down quite innocently, such as by dying on us, or some other unanticipated turn! So let your sense of forever-Being be your new comfort zone. How can this be put into practice? Be a Spiritual Warrior determined to do the inner work, knowing that the main enemy is you!! Examine your emotions and the underlying beliefs, thereby making the unconscious programming conscious so that you can examine it and change it for the better. Drop everything that is not you. Fight the good fight to eradicate negativity, unkind judgment and habitual resistance to what-is. Be the best that you can be for your sake - and for others in your presence!

It's important that your ladder of purpose is leaning against the right wall, so that your time and energy are put to good use.

Becoming Free

Be deliberate in living in the vertical dimension by shifting your attention. The shift you need, as described earlier in this chapter, can be expressed as "Loving POSE": Loving **P**resence, **O**neness (with Source, Space or Life), and **S**urrender to what-is, and **E**nough (or completeness; nothing needs to be added to the sense of self).

The acronym POSE is elaborated below:

Presence

1. Watch the thinker, the voice in your head, the self-talk, impartially without judgment

2. You are not the possessing entity – the thinker loses its power as you consistently observe it.

3. Be present, now, fully alert like the servant consciously awaiting his master's return

4. Use your body's inner energy field, the breath, or any object as an "anchor" that diverts attention away from mind-activity to provide peace *from* mind

5. Give your full attention to everything that you do, occasionally checking in with your anchor(s). In-between activities use your anchor(s) to maintain presence

6. Monitor, evaluate and improve your responses or reactions to situations arising

7. Move from *slave* to thought, to *observer* and transformer of unconscious thought and *author* of conscious thought

Oneness

1. Feel your connection with the eternal, the timeless, the un-manifested as mind activity subsides

2. Focus attention on the permanent, forever-Being dimension – the Kingdom of Heaven on Earth - what's the point in identifying with and developing the impermanent human ego?

3. Calm your thinking! Enter no-mind, (i.e. no self-talk), no-self, (i.e. realizing deeply that everything about the *physical* you including thoughts is temporary, fleeting), and be connected with timeless, eternal consciousness, free of judgment, attachment or any form of resistance to what-is

4. Realize the state of pure consciousness that utterly dwarfs your 5 senses, thoughts and emotions

5. Sense forever-Being in the people that you meet or associate with

Surrender

1. Surrender your old beliefs and conditioning to scrutiny – be prepared to renew your mind, employing new self-talk and imagery – for example, applying the acronyms "LUCKY-FACES-SCHOOL" covered in this chapter and focusing on love and gratitude, (Chapters 8 and 10 refer).

2. Spend time in silence. Perhaps ask the Creator or the universe what it would have you do and listen for and write down the answers. Similarly, ask the universe how to get what you want.

3. Commit "I don't mind what happens" and "this too shall pass" to memory, yet exercise preferences

4. Raise your vibration to joy through (a) surrender of ego to forever-Being and (b) mood-management

Enough

1. Know that you are enough already. Imagine other life forms having to defend a sense of self. In nature there is only acceptance and it's always now. Apply "FACES" to yourself.

2. You were created by, or through, the Creator, so there is no need to defend your existence or to ever feel less than enough. You are what you are and it could not be otherwise. You are more than enough!

Realize that we are an evolving species and perhaps you can play a part in raising consciousness, reducing suffering and helping others live freer and more fulfilled lives.

CHAPTER 8

Love

The Great Miracle of Life is Energy, which is to say life energy, which is to say love energy, which is to say Creation or manifestation formed by means of a continuous process of energy transformation.

While it is a fundamental rule of science, that energy can neither be created nor destroyed, there is abundant, perhaps limitless, infinite energy throughout the Universe. Of course, this is the great mystery, and beyond the capacity of human mind to understand.

In religious texts, we are commanded to "love God with all our heart, soul and mind" and to "love your neighbor *as* yourself." How can we love God or our Creator directly if we are unable to see or sense that? We can only do that by knowing and loving the Creator's creations and by heeding the rules of life provided by the greatest life-coaches that ever lived including, but not limited to, Jesus and Buddha.

Love is expressive, expansive, abundant and joyous. It is the energy that flows naturally and effortlessly from "forever-Being." An energy without polarity, unlike everything in the material world, that is full of contrasts, shades and opposites. We're not talking about romantic, needy love, or conditional or transactional "love." It is the very life force that is available to us evermore, as we open to it through surrender and acceptance – refraining from blaming or judging negatively, resisting, and clinging emotionally to people, events or situations. It is warm, appreciating and nurturing.

With reference to the Life Purpose Map shown below, *Joy, Contribution* to life and *Doing-no-harm,* (that correlate with authenticity), are pre-requisites for the joy of life to *flow naturally,* both within and without us.

THE LIFE PURPOSE MAP — LIFE FLOWS WHERE YOUR ATTENTION GOES!

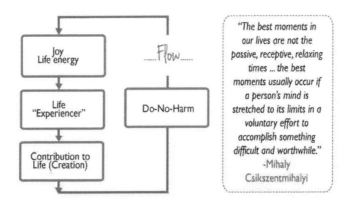

Joy, Life Energy

Eckhart Tolle writes in the Power of Now that *"nothing can give you joy. Joy is uncaused and arises from within as the joy of Being."* Jesus referred to the *"Kingdom of Heaven within,"* and advised to *"deny thyself"* which is to transcend the ego. And of course his greatest commandment was to love all. We can get a sense of this high vibrational joy by paying full attention to the present moment, and fully surrendering to and appreciating what is – attention to our forever-Being, the life force that permeates us, and that is provided to us, and all life forms, by the Creator.

Life Experiencer - Awareness

We are all life-*experiencers*, through our 5 senses, our thoughts and feelings, and our intuitions. When our ego is in check, and we are operating from our perspective of *forever-Being*, the love and *Joy* of life can *flow* through us naturally. We are surrendered to, and not resisting, life. Consistent with the expression "experiencer," a fundamental spiritual realization is that we are the *awareness*, the *observer* of what goes on through our senses and mental processing. So we can listen to the "voice in our head" – our thoughts, and sense our emotions, without being identified with them. This is the beginning of the end of the ego *as your controller*. And it is the start of living in *Awareness*.

As Experiencer, we should be either contributing to life, which means to create good things, or at least we do- no-harm, wherever practicable. We can contribute directly, through our choices, decisions and behaviors, and our thoughts have a tendency to become things. Our thoughts affect our bodies, something that you may know from personal experience. Albert Einstein is quoted as having said, "I admit that thoughts affect the body." And, your thoughts as an energy form, may affect your subsequent behavior, (as in the RAFTS Map), or be picked up by others, and possibly, acted upon.

Contributing to Life

Contributing to life is an essential component of this Life Purpose Map, and its absence may produce harm to self and others. So, if you're feeling less than brilliant or joyous, you may need to ask yourself "what am I contributing?" Even if you are currently going through some significant challenges in your life, this question may still be relevant, although your top priority is to deal with the challenges operating from a state of presence.

"Contribution to life" is intended to be through our expression of unique talents or calling. So spending a large part of our lives sitting in a cave, meditating in solitude doesn't cut it … unless we are also contributing to the (one) life, and can say with our hand on our heart that we are not hurting our self or others, that we are truly happy with our chosen vocation and environment.

Unless we contribute to life in a way that is meaningful to us, the *flow* will be inhibited – the life force energy permeating our every cell wants us to truly live. That's why it's there! Indeed, the evolutionary process never stops from moment to moment, and the myriad of automatic processes that happen in our bodies without any conscious effort on our parts is an example of that. And, at a much wider level, the entire universe is continuously, eternally, creating and transforming in every moment. And not only are we a part of the unfolding stupendous miracle of life, we always have been a part of it and always will be!

Now, it's really important that our *contribution to life* emanates from our authentic selves and not from ego!! Deciding what to do with our lives can be tricky, and is somewhat influenced by our conditioning, environment and natural inclinations. All too often, yet entirely understandably, we are motivated by the survival or security instinct and the need to accumulate or have access to sufficient money – a consequence of living and conditioning in this modern man-made world. So faced with a potentially boring, yet well paid technical job, or trying to survive in something we prefer such as an artist, actor or entertainer of some sort, we may be inclined to take the more secure path. We all know that only a small percentage of artists, actors, entertainers, etc. make any money, the rest are struggling to survive. Perhaps the ones making good money are the ones who love their work! Yet, it may not be that simple. It's easy to say *do what you love and the money will come* but it may be a false premise for many people. Or it may be true, yet *conditions apply,* such as having an identifiable market, and access to the technical and social abilities to serve that market. Many people are unable to meet these conditions or don't stretch far enough to engage the required resources.

So, how do we contribute to life, from our authentic or true selves? Some would advise to do what you love, regardless of the consequences, then you will have no regrets. That's fine so long as you're clear on what you love to do, and can adequately support yourself and any dependents financially. While it has become popular to advise to do what you love to do, there may be elements in pursuing a desired career that you do not like, and that you cannot easily change, at least in the short term. For example, you might have an overbearing ego-driven boss that you may have to sit out for a while, and learn to cope with. You might see this as "learning to cope with difficult people."

Having a *vision* for the future is helpful, although there are certainly people who have enjoyed a full life without a great deal of planning, and were only able to "connect the dots" of their growth on reflection many years later. There is something to be said in being *service-minded* while *doing what you can from where you are with what you have.* And this may apply whether you are born into wealth, comparative poverty or any other circumstance. Even if you are not working to make a living for whatever reason, you can still contribute in various ways to your family, friends and to your community.

Yes, you might say, but what about that bigger house and creating wealth? Can I do this from the forever-Being perspective? Essentially we all want to feel good in relation to ourselves and others; if you want something strongly, go for it and learn from it. You may want the big house for practical reasons or to make your ego-self feel more worthy or it may just be a preference to enjoy larger spaces. Only you can decide whether goals pursued are worthwhile based on your thoughts, feelings and experiences. Just remember your values and the desire to make a positive contribution.

The best way to contribute, to be your authentic self and to be fulfilled is, we are suggesting, to live your life, from the perspective of forever-Being. As we give, so we receive, so if you are a model of kindness, empathy and compassion, unfazed by any situation, (that is to say living as forever-Being), then you will be living in grace, and good things will always be about to happen! And, this will be true in the best or worst of situations in which you have choices to make.

Do No Harm

Now, about the "do-no-harm" component ... is this always possible? Suppose that you are in a physically or emotionally abusive or otherwise ill-fitting relationship that seems unchangeable? Getting out of it may hurt the other person

– it may hurt you too – yet it may be better for both of you in the fullness of time – with lessons learned by both. Of course, such relationships are better avoided in the first place, and the more authentic and conscious we are, the less likely we will be to err in our life choices. Then again, we can't always predict the future and perhaps sometimes we need to learn life lessons the hard way, as a meaningful part of our journey. Even if you're not responsible for a bad situation you are responsible for doing whatever you can to get out of it, if circumstances allow, responding consciously, or intelligently.

As covered in the previous chapter, in dealing with our life situations we need to practice **Love**, **Understanding**, **Compassion**, **Kindness** and Jo**Y** that can be remembered by the acronym LUCKY. More specifically in dealing with people, *starting with ourselves*, we need to practice **Forgiveness**, **Acceptance**, **Calmness**, **Empathy** and **Support** to wellbeing, encapsulated in the acronym FACES.

Flow – in touch with forever-Being and the Infinite

The *flow* that we feel, when this virtuous Life Purpose Map is operating, stems from the Creator's life energy and our non-resistance to life so that we go with the flow.

In order for this Map to operate there has to be both an inflow (Joy of life) and an outflow (Contribution to life). The inflow of joy can come when our *mood* is calm and alert/ bold and we are in a State of Surrender, operating from *forever-Being* rather than EGO (Edging God Out).

We can consciously increase our connection with love energy and joy by focusing on maintaining good moods, which can also be thought of as increasing our vibrational energy on Dr. Hawkins' Power versus Force scale. (See Chapter 1).

Ways to good vibes include:
- Appreciation and Acceptance: Loving what-is – from selective gratitude to all-encompassing appreciation for everything and everyone, (not forgetting yourself), – embodied as a way of life

- Authentic living in accordance with values
- Awareness, Oneness, Source-connection – meditation, mindfulness, forever-Being realization
- Conducive **environments** – e.g. nature, quiet cafes with good décor and "feel good" music, entertainments; whatever uplifts your mood
- Inspiring people, books, films, music, educational videos, works of art, etc.
- Good **relationships** with inner circle of family and friends
- Exercise, sleep, diet, relaxation
- Healthy finances

See also Chapter 10 on Gratitude which is related to flow and joy.

Blind Ambition of the Ego versus Meaning

We are all co-creators with God, or if you prefer, Mother Nature. If your birth was an accident, it was a pretty amazing accident! You were created as part of the awesome evolutionary process that has roots long, long, long ago. You have a temporary form component – human, and an eternal formless component – Being.

When we talk about *ambition*, we are talking about that desire to be great, to show to ourselves and the world what we are capable of achieving. Or, it may just be a strong desire for something that we think will make us feel good like a shiny new sports car or a new relationship with that sexy blonde or both! This is the human side of us perhaps sensing its vulnerability and wanting to be somebody. It is not entirely selfish yet it is primarily concerned with protecting me and mine. Others may love us for our achievements including proud family members and others who are pleased to be associated with our worldly status. We might reason, well I didn't ask to be here, yet here I am – I might as well make the most of it! Hmm now, what can I do to make this human existence enjoyable and worthwhile? What should I spend my time doing? Now what would I find fulfilling?

In my case, some of my experiences have included:

1. Becoming a civil engineer instead of a musician – an option in my early twenties

2. Gaining two graduate degrees in management reflecting interest in performance and creativity

3. Traveling the world – over 40 countries

4. Becoming a management consultant in the construction industry

5. Writing articles for the British Chamber of Commerce, in Indonesia, BritCham

6. Exercising daily – long term commitment

7. Playing guitar and writing songs

8. Multi-cultural and ethnic associations and experiences

9. Becoming a property investor

10. Becoming a book author and publisher

When we talk about *meaning*, we are talking about that desire to continue adding value and being purposeful while feeling good about what we are doing and the events surrounding us. This is the forever-Being side of us aware of its perfection, invincibility and completeness with nothing to prove. Yet, it's quite alright to tell your neighbor or friends about achievements or shortfalls in the right context while being sensitive to potential ego reactions that could arise if being boastful or concerned with one-upmanship. The right context would be a feel good one for all concerned.

Living from forever-Being perspective, you can never be diminished, because your essence is indestructible and as pure as light.

Compassion

Imagine that you are an eternal, feeling, intelligent alien with no prior knowledge of planet Earth. You arrive on Earth and see the human condition for the very first time and observe as follows:

(i) The short life span of humans, even 100 years is short compared to planet Earth (4.5 billion years) or compared to eternity itself, and does it *really* matter whether one lives 50 years or 100 years?

(ii) Pauper or Prince – all seem to suffer with varying levels of frustration and fulfillment; moreover none asked to be born!

(iii) Dominance of the ego arising from the frail human condition and sense of separation, with mild to severe mental afflictions ranging from anxiety to depression that trouble most people at one time or another

(iv) The manifestations of ego and sense of separateness – fear, lack, greed, naked ambition at any expense, striving for non-authentic goals, exploitation, wars, abuses of political and religious power, pursuit of more, more, more for its own sake, etc.

(v) Misdirection and herd mentality of many people including situations like the crucifixion of Jesus causing Jesus to say "forgive them, for they know not what they do"

Given these observations, an eternal, intelligent alien looking objectively at the human condition would have to feel compassion! That doesn't mean of course, that everything on planet Earth is in a mess, and there are a lot of good happenings playing out each and every day to take heart from.

Some things you might like to consider:

1   You didn't ask to be born (as far as you're aware?)

3.   So, you can say "I just Am," or "I Am" or "I Am that I Am" - now, we are not suggesting that you declare yourself as God, you are the created after all. Interestingly though, "I Am that I Am," is the phrase apparently used by God in response to Moses when enquiring as to His name. (Hebrew Bible, Exodus 3:14). In any case though, you're definitely part of a miracle!

4.   Since you did not ask to be born, and the Creator created you, your Creator or Source also plays a part in what comes out of you or how you show-up? How big a part?

5.   The Creator, that power behind the infinite space and universe(s), that created you through a sequence believed to include the "big bang,"

the formation of planet Earth, and a dazzling array of earlier life forms is much more powerful than your ego, (your sense of self as identification with your thoughts and emotions); much more powerful than that you can figure out through the wondrous, (yet limited), sense perceptions that you have as a human

6.   If you "deny thyself" – deny identification with, and slavery to, your thoughts and feelings then the powerful Creator can work through you more easily, enabling love, joy and increased consciousness. Experiment and see what happens …

7.   Increasing your vibrational level, your consciousness in higher realms from love upwards, would positively impact all around you and perhaps collective consciousness

8.   Imagine fully surrendering to the "perfection" of all that is; love all that is; resist nothing! No problems, no worries. You, (your essence), is still here, *no matter what* is going on around you, and will continue beyond your impermanent human form

Adventures

What does adventure mean to you? Our whole life is or should be an exciting adventure. Why settle for less? Our biggest adventures should arise from forever-Being, which is to say consciously chosen and free of any unhelpful conditioning or "baggage."

Coming from the state of being or presence we are alert, bold, calm, detached and engaged. And, operating from boldness, an adventure makes us feel and come alive. Create your own rules for life, with the caveats of contributing, doing-no-harm and living in the moment.

In our day to day living we can identify three main areas for living:
1. Mind-set – adventures of the mind – developing skills, systems and strategies for success
2. Moments – adventures in meaningful experiences and service – living a fulfilling, authentic life
3. Money – adventures in keeping our heads above water! – Passive income and financial freedom

These are all interrelated. *Mind-set* founded on qualities of the heart, growth and optimism will determine the scope of our vision, how intelligently we respond to the world in which we find ourselves, and how we feel about every aspect of our lives; *moments* refers to our life ventures, experiences, contributions and what we acquire and give back; and, *money* refers to that man-made practical resource for trade and exchange which funds our life adventures and creative pursuits. In the 3M Map below, the quality of our *mind-set* underpins our quality of life in terms of *moments* experienced or felt, and *money* received and utilized.

THE 3M MAP: LIFE THEMES AND FOCI OF ATTENTION

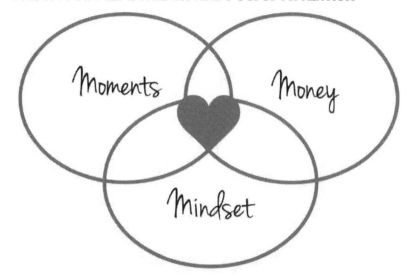

The "sweet-spot" represented by the heart in the center of the 3M Map, occurs when we apply optimal attention to each element of mind-set, moments and money to provide the most fulfilling results. Mind-set is the key foundational element, and moments is about your chosen lifestyle best spent living joyously day by day, moment to moment in love with life.

Now although "money" has been around for thousands of years, if you lived a few hundred years ago you may have only just witnessed the introduction of paper-money in your country. So, before then money wasn't available or relevant, only other assets such as land and livestock. Money is essential in this day and age, and there is nothing unspiritual about it, so long as it is acquired and used honestly. In line with the 3M Map, your best aim is to have sufficient passive income to live well.

You deserve a good life, not enslavement to work just to pay your bills and expenses.

Money funds your moments *and* your living expenses that may be intertwined. Family, accommodation and transport tend to be our largest expenses. You need to arrange your life in a way that makes you happy, and that may include simplifying your life. So if, for example, your finances are tight, you might consider relocating to somewhere that has lower living costs, or downsizing to repay a mortgage. If it's your dream to live in a large house in a lovely environment, that's fine too so long as the "sweet-spot" is maintained, and you're not killing yourself in the process. Only you can judge what's right for you, your situation and your vision.

Our greatest riches are found in our moments. Some people focus on money, some on moments, and some do both. In the traditional model, many people focus on money pre-retirement with the hope of enjoying money during retirement in their sixties … which sadly doesn't always come. And, unfortunately in saving and sacrificing until retirement, people can become more and more conditioned and confined to their comfort zone and limited daily routines, reinforcing old habits. Don't wait until your old-age to regret what could have been!

Some people focus on moments, for example based on traveling for months or years at a time, interspersed with months or years of work to make money to fund their future moments, or next adventure. Mini-retirements - a moments and money "sandwich."

Perhaps more people should cast security aside for a life of moments, living as forever-Being and a Spiritual Warrior. Yet, there is no guaranteed approach, and we never know when our number is up to meet our maker. The worst case scenario, is to live a highly stressed treadmill life of limited worthwhile achievement and little joy, perhaps compromising principles for a salary, to fit a dysfunctional work culture, then dying a week after retirement-day before getting a chance to enjoy spending the money!

The best case scenario, is living a life full of joyful exhilarating moments, where somehow sufficient money always arrives from whatever source to fund our wonderful lifestyle, while in the process, being a source of joy to others. Is this a chance worth taking? How big is your faith and imagination? What goals and dreams are you going to make happen, no matter what?!

Mind-Set Adventures – Skills, Systems and Strategies for Success

An Introduction to Living as a Spiritual Warrior: Keys to developing the mind-set of a Spiritual Warrior are living in Freedom, Love, Adventures (or experiences), Gratitude and Service (FLAGS). This embraces managing our mind and mood, and learning to live in the present while loving-what-is.

The way that you choose to live and respond to life, is a direct reflection of your mind-set. It is important then to "Know Thyself," a phrase often attributed to Socrates, and inscribed at the Temple of Apollo at Adelphi, Greece. "As within so without," and, "as above so below," are further ancient sayings that point to your external world being a reflection of your inner world. A Course in Miracles says that one day we will realize that nothing occurs outside our own minds.

If you want a great life, you will need to operate from forever-Being as a Spiritual Warrior and *renew your mind*. Indeed, "Be the change that you wish to see in the world" to quote Gandhi.

And, to renew your mind there are two **actions** that you must take:

1. Live in the light, the life energy, the life force of the Cosmos by living in the here and now moment, and *consciously* focusing on peace, love, joy and appreciation for all things.

2. Let go and allow the light in, to overcome the darkness or *unconsciousness* of your ego, unhelpful prior conditioning and associated limiting-beliefs, thoughts and emotions.

It is essential to recondition your beliefs, (things you feel to be true but may not be), because your beliefs are the dominant factor in determining your actions and results in life. Some of these beliefs are conscious, such as certain preferences, others are unconscious. Some beliefs are good for you, and others, generally referred to as limiting-beliefs, prevent you from living life to the full. Now, in order to change your limiting-beliefs you need to know what they are, and the way to find this out is to examine your self-talk and your emotions. As witness or observer, you are then in a position to correct or reframe the beliefs that you consider to be unhelpful or painful. Some negative emotions and fears will dissolve or dissipate under your observation. This is the Power of Awareness.

And, you must surrender all that is not you – this means temporary aspects including thoughts, emotions and some beliefs that come and go. Ultimately, your (ever-changing) body isn't you either, just a vehicle for this human lifespan.

It is very essential to apply this inner work.

Further, to be a Spiritual Warrior, confronting your demons or shadow-self, certain **understandings** are required:

1. You have a choice in developing a *mind-set and way of being* in the world that truly serves life, by allowing consciousness, the Creative Energy of Source, to flow through you unimpeded.

2. Everyone is living according to their current level of consciousness. Forgive unconsciousness! And, learn unconditional acceptance.

3. No one asked to be born! Be compassionate with yourself and others.

4. You were *created* just like a flower and the life force gives life without additional effort – the lilies neither toil nor spin – nor need you! Let go!!

5. You can accept that your digestion runs unaided, by the life force. Why force things? Relax!

6. You're safe!! There's no man-eating tiger in the room! Be calm and bold!

7. Death is never far away and is simply a milestone on your journey. Live one day at a time.

8. It is impermanence, (the temporary nature of forms), that makes everything possible within the context of inter-being and oneness

9. Do or die is an acceptable commitment to your few fervent passions/contributions

10. Practice makes perfect and repetition is the mother skill for rewiring beliefs and successful habits

Realize and remember that whenever negativity or uncomfortable emotions come up that you have inner work to do! Be (a Thought) and Emotion Detective!! What must you be thinking and believing for this emotion to arise? Question, correct, accept or change.

Train yourself to remain present in the now as much as possible, returning to your breath, or other *non-thought* aspect of attention. Relax, let go and love what-is. Be alert to your thoughts and feelings, catching any negativity in the bud, before it causes you or others trouble. Have faith in your eternal divinity, in your Oneness, (as the life force or consciousness, connected back to Eternity or Source through the preceding causal chain that includes the earliest human beings, the formation of our planet and the evolution of our universe – Introduction refers).

In awareness, you dis-identify with the time-bound ego that is lost in past and future. Fearless action is the key to all worthwhile success!! And this refers to love-inspired action from forever-Being, not from ego, or ultimately, fear-driven action! Your present moment acceptance of challenges when they arise, leads to the emergence of powerful and effective solutions. Refuse to be buffeted by life's storms that cannot ruffle your untouchable essence. You're still here.

Be relaxed, calm, bold and present at all times.

Some challenges just arrive out of the blue and we are "forced" into responding. Acceptance, then intelligent thought and action is needed when faced with challenges such as a death in the family, an unwelcome change in government legislation, the loss of an income stream, and many other challenging situations that may arise and sometimes without warning. Yet the greatest challenge we ever face is our response to events unfolding and this is where dis-identification with ego, story-lines and attachments is so important. Life goes on. Indeed life *is* change, so change is to be expected!

When faced with setbacks, put things in perspective and realize how lucky you are. In general, live your life enjoyably and enthusiastically, and recall the acronym "SCHOOL" which stands for Smiling, Confident, Happy, double-Optimistic, Lover of life.

Experience a sense of Oneness, live in the present in a state of surrender to the flow, and with an attitude of gratitude which is to love what-is, then you are bound to be more "LUCKY," recalling the acronym for being Loving, Understanding, Compassionate, Kind and joYful. And, from that place you will *feel good* and be fully engaged in this adventure of life.

Again, *always* act with boldness from a place of calmness, rooted in presence.

Mind-set and Meditation: Managing or taming the ego is one of the most important aspects in developing our mind-set. Associated therewith is the importance of paying *attention* to the present moment as opposed to being lost in perpetual thought and accompanying emotions concerning past or future.

Traditionally, meditation – present, non-judgmental *attention* on an object, typically the breath - has been the tool used to tame the ego. Left entirely to its own devices the mind can jump around in an undisciplined way that may not be in the best interests of its benefactor. Meditation then, is bringing discipline and purpose to the mind, taking it out of the automatic stream of thought, out of "monkey-mind." Meditation techniques can progressively calm the mind, emptying it of any stressful thoughts, providing access to forever-Being.

Yet, not everyone is fond of, or advocates traditional forms of meditation. Remember that the main point is to be present this very moment with a calm, undisturbed mind. Eckhart Tolle suggests placing our *attention* in the inner body energy field and, according to our preference, to take a few mini-meditations during each day – this can be something very informal and comfortable, whatever works for you and can be as simple as paying attention to a few breaths every now and again. Personally, I have never followed any of the detailed posture suggestions for meditation and advocate adopting a relaxed, care-free open physiology while sitting – like you belong and fit in perfectly with your surroundings. There are walking meditations too. The key thing is that you can make it a comfortable daily habit and that you feel calm, relaxed and present, surrendered to "what-is." If it feels comfortable to put a smile on your face go ahead and do that occasionally too.

So, you don't have to make a big thing out of meditating, simply breathe consciously in a relaxed and easy way whenever you can remember to do so. It *is* important that our minds are clear and calm, open and accepting, and that we are present in the here and now. And, as per above, we don't always have to use our breath as our object of meditation. Indeed, from a place of clear presence, it may be appropriate at times to choose to meditate on manifesting money or that sexy blonde instead! These *are* practical uses of our minds!! Seriously though, don't get attached, yet don't hold back from an adventure that you and others can enjoy and grow from.

We can distinguish between *inner adventures* and *outer adventures* corresponding to inner purpose and (inter-related) outer purpose. Our *inner purpose* is about realizing the person that we truly are, in our essence, which may be a process of discovery, and letting go of all that we are not; while our *outer purpose* is concerned with how we show up in the world – our *Doing*. Both inner purpose and outer purpose are concerned with the flow of *Joy*.

Mind-set and Mindfulness: We are sometimes advised to focus on our inner world for joy and happiness rather than our outer world. This may sound like a recipe for boredom if we have become accustomed to enjoying and relying on the many things that the external world has to offer. The Buddha pointed to pleasures as a source of suffering because of the inevitability of their impermanent and changing nature which can lead to a sense of loss and suffering if we are attached to those pleasures and associated objects of pleasure. Yet, the adage "everything in moderation" may be an adequate antidote, (and consistent with what Buddhists call "the middle way"); after all we have to eat, for example, (which is a source of pleasure). Furthermore, we can enjoy many other things *provided that we are not addicted to them.*

So, enjoy the externals, indeed (co)-create a wonderful life with the intention of doing no harm and adding to life, (not your ego or sense of self). Just be aware that whatever you possess, *and* cling to, possesses you, and that the conditions for your happiness, don't require you to struggle or to be rich financially. There's no need to compare yourself with others. And learning to appreciate the good things in life, using the senses that our Creator provided us, may require you to shift your attention to a simpler yet more fulfilling lifestyle. We were given our senses for a reason – to utilize them! Don't forget!

Mindfulness, (defined by Jon Kabat-Zinn as paying attention in a particular way, on purpose, in the present moment, and non-judgmentally"), teaches us not only to pay attention to, but to *savor*, to enjoy and find pleasure in whatever we are doing in the present moment. Benefits of living in mindfulness, include:

1 Increased feelings of relaxation and calmness
2 Improved mood and alertness
3 Increased concentration and focus
4 Greater self-awareness and insight
5 Feeling more in touch with purpose and meaning
6 Better ability to cope with adversity
7 More accepting of self and others
8 More sense of space and less mental-noise
9 Life feels more fulfilling
10 Greater appreciation of one's life
11 Increased ability to cope with pain or illness

If you slip up, and serve your own ego occasionally, it's not the end of the world – you're a *human* being after all! And, we haven't yet reached the collective New Heaven and Earth cited in both the Old and New Testaments of the Bible, which some equate with the flowering of consciousness in human beings, as part of the human evolutionary process.

Do enjoy the simple things in life through indulging in "moments."

Moments

Your time here on planet Earth as a human being is a very unique experience and opportunity handed to you. How will you make the most of it? What will your adventures be? Looking back to the "D Map," what is your life's destiny?

We are here to experience joy and feel good, and in order for that to be the case, we must be fully engaged in the stream of life. And, a prerequisite is to be confident and happy now.

"Follow your bliss" suggests Joseph Campbell. It is important to live life on your own terms, to live your own life, not the life that others would have you live. And it is important to your healthy realization and wellbeing to live as far as possible without needy or clingy attachments. This applies most particularly to the approval of others. Imagine how freeing it is never to have to worry about the good opinion of others! You can still listen to people who truly have your best interests at heart. And, you can still cooperate authentically with others, yet at times you may need to say "no" (diplomatically) so that you can focus on the right priorities.

Well, it would be nice if we only ever had feel good stuff in our lives. Living authentically, being bold, calm and present will keep us in the flow of joy much of the time. And, do not forget to support your wellbeing and energy levels through quality exercise, diet and sleep.

In the context of working, according to Alan Watts, "This is the real secret of life — to be completely engaged with what you are doing in the here and now. And instead of calling it work, realize it is play." So what moments do *you* want to create?

- Travel the world
- A University education
- Bringing up a functional family
- Being with your soul-mate with shared values
- Living in a great healthy environment and climate
- A great career doing work that you love
- An entrepreneur doing work that you love
- A super fit physique and tons of energy for life
- "Toys" – home, holiday home, car, boat, exotic holidays, …

Mere garnering of possessions for their own sake is not important. Yet it's alright to enjoy people and things in moderation, provided we do not get caught up in the "jar" of judgment, attachment and resistance arising from ego. Of course, any material wealth that we share during our life or that we bequeath to our loved ones may provide some opportunities for happiness. Yet in the end, how we feel, and how we tend to make others feel, is more important than anything else, and this does not in any way exclude the wise use of money and materialism. We're here to enjoy while doing no harm and if we can add to life rather than just pump up our frail ego then we can live a full life

In dealing with externals, the world of form, Eckhart Tolle's suggestions are pertinent:

- Outer purpose (worldly success) will matter as long as you haven't realized your inner purpose. After that the outer purpose is *just a game that you may continue to play simply because you enjoy it.*"
- Once we have our inner purpose sorted out and we are living authentically from being, then the outer purpose will take care of itself automatically.
- "The sooner that you realize that your outer purpose cannot give you lasting fulfillment the better. Give up unrealistic expectation that it should make you happy … every outer purpose is doomed to fail … because it is subject to the law of impermanence …"
- Become a participant in the play of form by creating without self-seeking; when you create without self-seeking, you'll create beautiful-

ly. However, when you create and there's self-seeking in it—when you tell yourself "I need," "I want," or "I must have"–, then you infuse the creative energy that is flowing through you with negativity.

- You'll live in a state of continuous joy, no matter what arises, when you realize that what arises isn't that important. What arises is just consciousness playing with form.

- The power of consciousness flows through you, and it loves to create; simply let it flow.

At the end of our very short human lives, (short compared to Mother Earth for example), our human form goes to dust and all of our achievements and possessions may not be all that important. Yet we need remember with gratitude that since the *stone-age*, and beyond, our familial ancestors have strived to improve the *quality of life* for succeeding generations thereby providing our generation with many comforts and conveniences that we can easily take for granted. So perhaps an ideal life would entail having a really great and joyful time while paying forward with a legacy that helps others to live easier, happier and more fulfilling lives.

Our needs for sustenance aren't really that great and many of us could simplify our lives. It pays to have thought through who you are, and what you really, really value and want out of life.

Your top priority is wellbeing, to feel good which will include great relationships with all the people that you value in your life. Can you flip the switch to the State of forever-Being and live in grace? After that you can enjoy playing the game of life while not taking things too seriously.

Life *is* experiences is moments. Enjoy and build a life that makes you overflow with gratitude and joy. Perhaps it's time to make your bucket-list if you don't have one already. These are the things and experiences that aren't necessary for your sense of completeness, yet you know will make your heart sing. This can include seasonal lists, for the summer or winter months, for example. Declare every fresh day with "Happy New Day!" and live moment by moment!

Money and Materialism

Perhaps if you had been born 3,000 years ago, money would not be important. In the real or practical world that human beings have evolved to, money is important. It's just the world environment that we have all been born into in the 21st century, where this practical man-made resource called money is needed for accommodation, travel and the basic necessities of life. As the old adage goes, I've been rich and I've been poor and believe me rich is better! Or consider the wisdom that becoming one of "the poor" doesn't help you or them!

It's true that once you really experience that which you truly are, ego-driven material demands based on lack, better-than, etc. will lessen or cease altogether. There is nothing to prove to your ego-self or anyone else. But that doesn't mean that you have to shun a nice house, car, holiday experiences and so on. Moderation in all things will serve you well whether it's food, alcohol, sex, sleep, exercise, travel or materialism of any kind. And, ideally, we would optimize our resources putting them to work harmoniously and efficiently. This can include our own talents, time, money or anything else at our disposal. So if for example you had surplus cash in the bank, it could be put to work to benefit yourself and others.

Do make sure that you organize passive income for yourself and any dependents so that money is available to you whether working or not. Don't be an unwilling slave to any occupation that, even with your positive attitude, is not serving your happiness.

People are often critical of spiritual teachers, (even sincere and credible ones), who have acquired wealth, implying that spirituality and wealth are mutually exclusive. Yet we can simply see this as the law of giving and receiving at work. Most genuine spiritual teachers provide a lot of free information in addition to potentially valuable but more expensive information provided by way of seminars, lectures or coaching. And, many of these teachers may be able to use their wealth wisely and in a well-intentioned manner.

Besides, expecting things to be free can suggest an entitlement mentality, albeit our Creator has provided a universe of amazing diversity and abundance for free. Yet, we all have to contribute to life, if we are to live in the flow of giving and receiving. This even applies to those born into riches and who could live their whole lives while hardly lifting a finger. We must give to live. And that doesn't automatically mean money, it can be time, wisdom, selfless nurturing, expertise, etc.

Consistent with "Contribution," *service,* (which is covered in Chapter 11), is something that flows through us out into the world. With forever-Being as the primary focus of attention in our lives we can be a source of joy to others and happy and content ourselves too. Alert, Bold, Calm, Detached and Engaged, helping people associated with us to lead happier lives would qualify as legacy from forever-Being.

Our purpose and legacy needs to shine through our forever-Being, not obscured by ego. It's quite likely that no one will remember you 20 years after your death. And this is a very, very short period of time indeed compared to human evolution!!

CHAPTER 10

Gratitude

G ratitude has been called the secret of life. Now, this may seem a rather tall claim if we have only understood "gratitude" at a superficial level, from our everyday experience of the use of this word. At the positive end of the spectrum, the word "Gratitude" may give rise to feelings of abundance and awe of life, while at the opposite end, it may make people question whether they have been grateful enough, and actually invoke guilty feelings. Of course, in this book, we are encouraging you to sense gratitude from the former perspective.

We can get to a deeper sense of what is meant by gratitude, if we think of it as choosing to like or love what-is, which is to give warm acceptance and appreciation for all things, and to say a resounding yes to the flow of life. Byron Katie has written a whole book entitled "Loving what is."

Gratitude can be connected to all the other "FLAGS" values, for example to "Freedom" through being at peace with, and accepting the present moment; to "Love," through reverence for what-is; to "Adventures," through appreciating experiences such as a sunset or an inspiring concert; and, to "Service" through appreciation of giving and receiving.

Gratitude is a form of **attention**. Shining our light of awareness on the good in our life ... and it's all good in the fullness of time if we can learn to see through the eyes of gratitude ... even mishaps have their lessons and eventually their blessings, if we look for them.

From the time that we first awaken, to the time that our heads hit the pillow, we need to live from a background of *Presence* or *forever-Being*, with *gratitude* as our default emotion when not otherwise engaged in meaningful, present moment pursuits that include rest, relaxation and renewal.

We are all one with Source. We all came from the same place, all forged from the same elements, all interdependent and inter-Being with the sun, the earth, the oceans (water) and space (air). Gratitude for our brief sojourn on Planet Earth is fundamental.

One day, your formless essence will leave your corpse and then there will be new adventures – what happens next is not yet clear to us, although there are many accounts of Near Death Experiences (NDE), where people have had a sense of transitioning on to the next stage of life, and have described their experiences positively, including losing the fear of death in some cases. So you can be grateful in anticipation of the mysteries of your post-death experiences.

As we go about our daily lives, we are generally motivated either by fear of what we don't want, or desire of what we do want. Living in appreciation and gratitude is consistent with the loving, as opposed to the potentially fearful part of us, keeping us on the side of the angels. What we appreciate, appreciates (or grows). When we're in a grateful mode, we are expressing the feeling of happiness for what is going right in our lives, at the level of be, do and have. Law of attraction advocates will tell you that this will attract more of the same – and that this is a form of abundance. In fact, abundance is anything that makes you *feel good*, and goes well beyond receiving financial abundance. Would you rather be a miserable millionaire addicted to money while sensing significant lack in certain areas of life or be a joyous junkie living with true love and seeing nothing but abundance and Oneness? Of course you may be both a millionaire and a joyous junkie, both conventionally successful and spiritual, which is great.

As mentioned in the Introduction, we need to live in a State of Love, Joy and Gratitude as advised by the Buddha, and more than 2,500 years ago.

Does Joy Lead to Gratitude?

Now what comes first in order of our feelings, joy or gratitude? Dr. Brene Brown has drawn attention to science-based research that concludes, that while people may tend to think that gratitude arises from joy, it occurs the other way round. For more information visit her website www.brenebrown.com where she explains that "it is gratitude that makes us joyful."

Indeed, the research suggests that gratitude leads to joy. This at first sight seems at odds with spiritual teachings that joy is uncaused, coming from within. Perhaps the difference can be explained by realizing that comparatively few people feel connected to Source, (and thus joy, aliveness), while most others are operating primarily from ego except in rare moments. Operating from ego, one is by definition subject to potentially endless anxieties associated with separation, self-protection, me and mine. Changing state and emotional vibration by diverting attention from anxious thoughts, to thoughts of gratitude, will make people feel better and more inclined to joy. It is not difficult to see why gratitude is at the heart of spirituality.

As *forever-Being,* one sees perfection in creation and accepts, indeed surrenders to reality or "what-is" – which is surrender to the Creator, or put another way is simply getting ourselves out of the way so that our Creator can work or flow through us unimpeded. Consistent with this, is to love what-is, always and without condition, which is gratitude for everything in one's perception of reality this moment. In expressing unconditional love and gratitude, we are simultaneously surrendering to "what-is." Uncaused joy, and gratitude for all that-is, may merge into one feeling from *forever-Being* perspective. *Forever-Being* is one with the one-life and Source of all creation. This discussion is consistent with the SHIFT Map introduced in Chapter 7, and the Life Purpose Map in Chapter 8.

What are we Grateful for?

As human beings we know the world according to our particular set of sense perceptions, which are different from other life forms. (Incidentally, this tells us that we only see the *particular reality* as it appears to the genus of human beings, not the full reality of life). We perceive through our 5 senses, and our mind-body processes of thought, feeling and consciousness.

Unless you work in a perfumery perhaps and it's your job to smell out the quality of fragrances, the physical senses that you use *most of the time* will be *seeing* and *hearing,* assuming that these senses are not significantly impaired. Nevertheless, we would significantly miss the senses of smell, taste and touch if absent. Then we have mind-associated *thoughts,* and *feelings* felt in our body. And we have our formless "life force," which we may feel as a subtle energy field and notice as our "*awareness* of awareness," that we have had since birth. Our *forever-Being.*

We can feel gratitude for all good things that we see and hear, the taste of various foods and drinks, the smell of flowers or coffee or freshly baked bread, and sensing the touch of so many things from our door key and the coins in our pocket, to the texture of our relaxing armchair.

Yet you may say, "this is all great, and I really, really do appreciate it ... but what's the real thing?!" Well loving what-is, is the real thing. Our Creator or God gave us particular senses, not only to survive and outwit wild bears, but also to utilize for our wellbeing and enjoyment. Wrapped up in our minds we can fail to know the beauty all around us. With our specific God-given senses we can also enjoy and feel gratitude for sunsets, rainbows, incredibly beautiful marine life in clear waters, great books, works of art, the incredible variety of music and all manner of things designed by humans from cars to houses to technological devices, etc.

Health is wealth and that should be a top priority, especially spiritual health.

Even, if at some time, your life situation *seems* dire, if you're reasonably healthy and able to live to a reasonably ripe age, what does it matter?

By all means schedule time to brainstorm solutions to your life situation issues but treat it as a game not something to worry over. Make a decision today – you will live every moment in gratitude, and as close as you can be to joy and bliss. Steadfastly refuse to let anything steal your joy.

By this point, you may be wondering about *love* in the context of relationships, which can be tricky as the ego's relationship with love tends to be needy and transactional. Never-the-less, relationships can be our greatest source of satisfaction and happiness if all is going well. The opposite is also true, and our perspectives on relationships that are not meeting our needs can be the cause of our greatest suffering. The Dalai Lama states in his book A Profound Mind, "I don't think that family and friends can ultimately provide the true inner happiness we seek. Loved ones often bring more anxiety into our lives, while a calm and peaceful mind imparts a profound happiness ..."

So ultimately, as we have made reference to throughout this book, getting fully in touch with your *eternal* awareness, oneness with Source, presence and joy, living in gratitude - *loving what-is, unconditionally* – will provide the fulfillment that you and everyone desires. *Irrespective of any of your religious affiliations* consider, again, the wisdom of Jesus Christ, the ultimate "life-coach" advising us of our top priority to love, (feel gratitude for), our Creator with all our heart, soul and mind; then love our neighbor *as* our-self perhaps signaling the common essence and Oneness of Life. How can we know the Creator or God? By the multiverse, universe, all creations and your faith in the unfathomable, unexplainable, in full awareness that you were created from a chain of events that extends back billions of years, perhaps eternity. As noted in Chapter 2, bear in mind that we wouldn't expect an ant to understand a human being, so it is that we human beings cannot comprehend our Creator other than through a reverence for all. As previously intimated, when Jesus Christ said that we could only know the Creator through him, perhaps he meant simply, that we need to follow his teachings or laws of life because we cannot know our Creator directly.

After all, "He" or" She" or "That" is not a wise man with a flowing beard, a tangible object that we can see with our amazing, (yet still limited), range of senses.

Ultimately a happy life requires that we live from gratitude. Then, we don't merely express gratitude, we are it. Gratitude *is* love!

What might you be grateful for? You can be grateful for your parents or caregivers who fed and clothed you for free; your education that may have been free; opportunities and valued acquisitions leading you up to the present day; Planet Earth and this amazing Universe, the air that you breathe, mighty oceans, mountains, galaxies and sunsets; a roof over your head; running water and electricity courtesy of your ancestors; and particularly the good things you can recall from the last day or so. Take nothing for granted!

While our sense of gratitude will vary according to our particular life experiences, and our attitude, we can identify various avenues of appreciation based upon our human perceptions as tabled overleaf.

Now, how many of these varied avenues of appreciation need money?

Yes, you will need funds if you want to visit the great wonders of the world, or go to see a musical or a concert, yet many things we desire are less about money, and more about getting off our butts to make things happen.

So long as you're alive and breathing, you have so much to be grateful for. Relax, surrender and let *it*, (mind-stuff), all go. Love what-is and make a decision to live in the light, in joy and enthusiasm, always.

Your Creator made you, so let the Creator's energy work through you. Get out of your own way, drop everything and let the Creator take care of it while stepping towards your goals and dreams.

PERCEPTION	EXAMPLES OF AVENUES FOR APPRECIATION
Eyes	To see beauty, to read books, see the wonders of nature, people, films, etc.
Ears	To hear people, nature, music, etc.
Nose	To smell freshly brewed coffee, baked bread, flowers, fruit, etc.
Mouth	To taste nice food, drink
Touch	Surroundings, people, door and car keys, nature, artefacts and furnishings
Legs/ feet	To walk, run, climb and get around
Arms/ hands	To hold, hug, write, type, eat, etc.
Thoughts/ *mind*	To consciously choose and co-create our lives; tame and train our thoughts
Feelings/ *heart*	To inform our decisions and actions – to feel good and love what-is
Awareness of awareness	To know the miracle of eternal life energy within and without us; to sense the one background formless stillness out of which everything arises; to see the sacred in all things; to see the blindness of the ego cocoon that keeps us trapped in illusion and out of touch with the reality of the moment

An element of the human condition is that we tend to take the familiar for granted. We may groan about some perceived lack in our lives, while ignoring the freely available abundance all around us – such as the plentiful supply of air that we breathe, the beautiful views if we choose conducive environments. There is a whole universe out there, perhaps many universes of awesome pro-portions. We all need to spend time on focusing on what's good as Saint Paul advises in Philippians 4.8.

And, you don't need to be a billionaire and have your own exotic island, (alt-hough that's great if you do and truly enjoy it). There are so many beautiful parts of this planet to see and appreciate. Imagine though, the irony of feeling trapped on your very own island that you paid a small fortune for ... when there are so many varied beautiful things to see and experience on our planet for free!

Benefits of Gratitude

There has been a lot of research by Professor Robert Emmons and others as well as the emergence of *positive psychology* over the last couple of decades. (Robert Emmons book, *Thanks! How Practicing Gratitude Can Make You Happier, 2008* details the research and findings of his work).

Gratitude has been found to help in healing, energizing and changing lives. Benefits are psychological, physical and social. Psychological benefits identified include more positive emotions, alertness, energy, enthusiasm, optimism, and better focus of attention. Physical benefits identified include 10-15% lower blood pressure in one study, the tendency to engage in more exercise, better sleep, and more attention to maintaining good health. Social benefits identified include better relationships and more inclination to help others.

It is worth commenting that the research has focused on gratitude as a single variable, albeit a very important one. Operating from forever-Being is a more holistic approach that goes well beyond gratitude as a single variable.

Practicing Gratitude

Unless you have already developed strong presence, emanating gratitude and joy naturally from the discipline of being in touch with your Being, you may need to make a start by spending time in *selective* practice of gratitude as opposed to an all-embracing attitude of gratitude. The Gratitude Map below shows varying degrees of gratitude related to the "4 Modes of Awareness" covered in Chapter 7, in the sub-section "Moving from the Prison of Victimhood to the Freedom of Presence."

THE GRATITUDE MAP: FOUR LEVELS OF GRATITUDE CORRESPONDING TO THE FOUR LEVELS OF AWARENESS

Forever-Being dominant	3. Accepting *Choosing gratitude consciously*	4. Awakened *Loving all-that-is habitually*
Ego dominant	1. Victim *Ungrateful*	2. Empowered *Selective gratitude*

There's no doubt that gratitude improves your attitude and mood. Many people keep a daily gratitude journal, typically recording 5 events in the day that went right for them or that they were able to appreciate. The very act of doing this can make people more aware of opportunities to be grateful for throughout their days. At some point during the day, you might say to yourself, for example, I know what's going into my gratitude journal later on! You might decide to go for the one thing, three things or just whatever came up which might result in a small list one day and a long list another day.

The best approach to gratitude journaling is to do whatever works for you, and if it feels forced at all, you need to re-evaluate your approach. If you find daily journaling difficult, try weekly or other regular intervals. It's important that you really do *feel* gratitude rather than merely engage the left brain in writing a list!

Yet our ultimate purpose is to live, matter of course, as *forever-Being* in the present, without judgmental stories, attachments and resistance of the mind or ego. Then our natural state is joy and gratitude for all things – loving all that-is, unconditionally. The natural flow of love-energy is unimpeded by the ego-mind. Beautiful flowers grow out of the mud, and it is the mind that draws distinctions between beauty and ugliness. The holistic gratitude of loving all that is without condition that we are referring to here, takes us from *conditioned unconsciousness* of the ego to the *non-conditioned consciousness* of forever-Being. And part and parcel of this level of gratitude, is non-resistance and surrender to *what-is.*

So rather than use the word *gratitude,* which tends to be selective, you may prefer to simply love *all* that is, always and unconditionally. This goes well beyond selective gratitude and is a way of being. If we can make this a habit it will really help us to make the shift from ego to forever-Being.

If we can move from selective gratitude, to an all-embracing, deliberate, conscious loving of all-that-is, then this all-encompassing gratitude can be easily related to other positive feelings. These feelings include love, joy, happiness, compassion, kindness, acceptance and forgiveness. We can be more understanding and empathic of unconscious people, if coming from an attitude of gratitude and presence. Einstein reportedly expressed gratitude a hundred times a day, so perhaps gratitude helped enable his insight, imagination and scientific achievements. *Giving* gratitude and *receiving* positive manifestations go together. And, we can know it from our own experience.

And, if you happen to know or follow that highest commandment to love God with all your heart, then realize that loving all (His/ Her) creations, appreciating them, and having gratitude for literally everything is perhaps the best way to achieve this.

CHAPTER 11

Service

S ervice is about the *quality of our attention, how* we serve or treat others, our attitude towards people and situations. Service is about giving and responding positively, about love rather than obligation. It's about inspiring and enabling, leading and supporting. And, the greater the number of people impacted positively, the better.

Jesus, Buddha and Gandhi, are people that many of us can relate to, as being of service to many. Service is a call not to take ourselves so seriously, and to remember the collective, the oneness, the whole of which we are all a part. Spread joy to the world.

Engaging in the art of present moment mindfulness, is one way to help ensure the quality of your attention and concentration on whatever activities you are purposefully engaged in. This aligns with the wisdom of the saying that "how you do one thing is how you do everything," with the implication that we should endeavor to bring a certain quality of perfection to whatever we do.

This is not a call for perfectionism, but to be fully absorbed in what we are doing, rather than being detracted by mental noise. In a performance event of any kind, the fear of appearing foolish, for example, or even thoughts about the importance of the result or potential reward, would take your focus off of the more important aspect of the quality of your doing this moment, which is the sole determinant of the quality of the result in a given context or situation.

THE RRRR (4R) MAP – RESOURCES, RECIPE, REWARDS, RELATIONAL CONTEXT

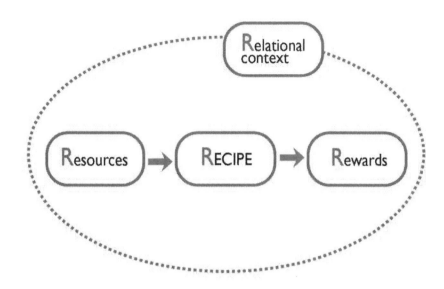

The RRRR Map shows that central to manifestation is the *RECIPE* – just like baking a cake, the recipe is the process for transforming *resources*, (such as people, ideas, materials, equipment, money, etc.), into *rewards*, (or results such as a delicious cake, a soul-mate, or a holiday in an exotic destination). Evidence from martial arts and spirituality, suggests that, focus on carrying out the recipe *in the* moment, rather than the rewards, will provide the best results. [That said, *design* of a recipe to assure quality of outcomes would be solely concerned with ensuring that the desired result is achieved consistently, every time].

Summarizing, we design, (or copy or refine), the recipe with care to ensure that the required result or specification will be achieved. Once we have the right recipe, we focus all of our attention in carrying it out meticulously, without detraction, (unless of course, something rather more important comes up). In common day usage, the *recipe* can be the automated "system" or "habit" or routine" or "ritual" we employ to manifest the results we are seeking. [Chapter 12 covers the important subject of habits in more detail].

Service to Wider Humanity

Service to humanity recognizes that we are *one* in the sense of inter-being, and this can take us away from any ego-selves and concerns that we may have. It's a recognition that there is a whole world out there. Indeed, there is a universe, (or even multiverse), of unfathomable extent of which we have limited perception, with our half a dozen human senses – and we are holding the mantle, oh so briefly, for our generation.

If we turn our thoughts to whom of our ancestors or contemporaries have contributed most to humanity, we will have to look at areas like health, technology, spirituality, careers, personal development, sport, and the arts. In thinking this through, you might want to consider what it is that *you* could contribute to mankind.

We have discussed the role of passive income in supporting our lifestyle. People with significant wealth are in a unique position to contribute to humanity, and help eliminate the causes of suffering on this planet.

Now, we can't all be Nobel Prize winners or big philanthropists financing worthy causes, yet you may be able to come up with a compelling vision for something that is feasible for you. Some people have achieved "impossible" dreams, (such as flight and artificial light), and as the great life-coach Jesus taught, as to your faith it will be done unto you. In the popular Law of Attraction, it is not only our thoughts on what we can manifest, but *the belief that we can,* that is so crucially important. Indeed, it has often been the limiting beliefs buried in our subconscious that have sabotaged our attainment of goals. Even better than belief is a real sense of *knowing,* and this is something that some personal development practitioners emphasize in spiritual and manifesting contexts.

Service and forever-Being

What is service but living from forever-Being, living from the heart? Our purposes will come to us, if this hasn't happened already, and everything we do in service of those purposes, should be infused with freshness and vitality. Being the change and thereby raising our own consciousness is key.

How much energy do we have to *give*? We might just as well say, how much energy do we have to *receive* from our Creator, once we get out of our own way? This second option might sound better to you, especially if you're feeling less than energetic right now!

The less we waste our mind-energies on detractions, on mental-noise, and the more we are aligned with certain higher energies referred to by Jesus, Buddha, Saints, indeed all spiritual people, and exemplified in David Hawkins Power versus Force typology mentioned in Chapter 1, the more potential-energy for achieving good we will have. We are talking about love, joy, appreciation, peace; living in the light as opposed to living by the darkness of ego, which is living from fear. We need to be in the flow of our Creator, our original Source, sensing our inter-connected essence, that difference between our current self and our corpse discussed in the Introduction of this book.

Forever-Being stands for freedom, love, adventures, gratitude and ... Service! What style of service inspires you? Consider the following and how they make you feel:

- Someone's refreshing and extraordinary kindness towards you or others
- A poor person giving away what little they have
- A champion overcoming the odds to secure victory
- Receiving sincere appreciation for service rendered
- Someone who reinvents themselves in a positive and moralistic way, and pulls their family into a higher social and economic status with positive benefits to society
- Stories of rags to riches through worthy means and laudable outcomes

These demonstrations of service have the potential to fill us with wonder and awe not dissimilar to a moment of solitude gazing into the still night sky of beauty while sensing the infinite space that is somehow part of us.

PART 3: Living Practices

CHAPTER 12

The HIVE Map: Habits-Imagination-Values-Expression

In order to get the most out of the contents of this book, it is important to commit to *practices* that will consolidate the material and enable you to *be the change* and live a full life. Can anyone ride a bicycle, drive a car or learn to swim by just reading about it?

I hope that you have enjoyed what you have read so far, that it resonates with you in some way, and that you have found the guiding frameworks and acronyms – life Maps – helpful. Yet, while this intellectual understanding will stand you in good stead, commitment to *practices* will help you reap the benefits of a full life, well beyond mere understanding. It has been said that to know something and not apply it is practically the same as not knowing it. As we have reinforced with the RAFTS and FLAGS Maps, actions and behaviors need to take place before we reap the benefits!

Key to authentic change for the better is developing powerful *Habits*, exercising our *Imagination*, consolidating our beliefs in terms of personal *Values* to live by, and *Expression* of our unique calling and talents. "Don't die with the music still in you" ... as the saying goes! These keys can be summarized by the acronym **HIVE** described overleaf.

Habits – routines, rituals, results

Imagination – life design, intention, thought experiments, examine and change beliefs/ habits

Values – those things we hold dear which *if accurately discovered* should inform, guide and even govern our choices. (E.g. **F**reedom, **L**ove, **A**dventures, **G**ratitude and **S**ervice as used in the "HIVE Map" below).

Expression – of our calling and unique talents providing self-satisfaction, fulfillment and help to others.

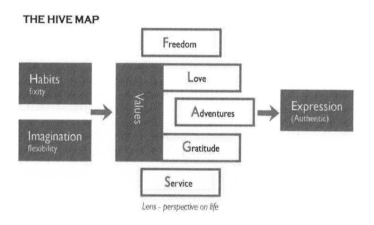

THE HIVE MAP

Habits

In the HIVE Map, habits are like the programs or software of the subconscious mind. Habits to a substantial degree run our lives and can literally make or break us. We have habits for sleeping, thinking, feeling, reading, speaking, socializing, listening, watching TV programs, travelling, shopping, working, eating, drinking, hobbies, organizing our affairs, commitments, decision-making, discipline, risk-taking, investing, spending and so on. The question arises then as to which habits best help us in our quest for a happy and fulfilled life. This is to some extent an individual thing, reflecting personal preferences, and we may all have a mix of good and bad habits. Many of our habits formed as we grew up in line with, or in reaction to, family and societal conditioning.

First we make our habits, (through a simple process of **repetition**), then our habits make us. Yet, the fact is, we often pick up habits unconsciously rather than deliberately creating them. So, rather than merely being a slave to our habits it is better to review them, both good and bad and if necessary improve them. This may mean eliminating bad habits that do not serve us, cultivating new ones that do, and reinforcing, (doing more of), our good habits. In order to live really fulfilling and meaningful lives, we need to consciously forge our habits through repetition in a state of still presence. This takes an average of 66 days according to research from University College, London in year 2009.

Your habits need to be directed towards two things – firstly, your wellbeing and happiness as your natural high energetic state and secondly, living the life of your dreams, doing things that you love to do, things that are important to you. This is what we all want really, yet the route is different for everyone mirroring our unique personalities, purposes, needs, values, strengths and preferences.

Another important thing is that we have a reliable income that supports our desired lifestyle. Now for a certain percentage of people, the traditional route of a job and pension may suffice. But, wouldn't it be nice, even if you truly love your job, to have sufficient income whether working or not? Acquiring income producing assets that provide passive income, (that is to say income received whether you work or not), may be your route to financial independence and freedom.

As intimated above, a well-lived life then, often requires **unlearning** and **stopping** some things in favor of focusing on higher value activities. Related thereto, we can all benefit tremendously from practicing daily rituals or habits that help propel us forward in the direction of our dreams. Our very life comprises our daily routines, habits and rituals. Even small shifts in our habits can lead to dramatically different results in our lives. [Useful analogies include the large final destination shifts that would arise from just a small change in the angle of striking a golf ball or a small adjustment to the rudder setting on a ship].

Before we move on to considering which useful habits you may want to adopt in living a full life, let us briefly look at how habits develop and how they may be changed. Habits are formed by repetitive behaviors that lead to strengthening neural pathways in our brains, a bit like thickening of a wire or cable, or you might prefer to think of it as leading to a deepening groove. Generally there is a 3 stage process in habit formation starting with a cue or trigger (e.g. oh it's 11am, it must be coffee time), then the *execution* of the habit, (drinking your coffee), then receiving the reward (enjoying the smell, taste and effects of your caffeine top-up).

In order to change or replace a habit it helps to recognize or identify the 3 stages mentioned above and ideally you find a better reward. You may also question and denigrate the previously perceived attractiveness of a habit that you want to change. Someone quitting the habit of smoking for example, may replace the smoking habit with a health and fitness habit. This could involve getting emotionally engaged in all the benefits of the healthy, strong, energetic and confident new you while imagining all the very real and dire perils of smoking to your quality of life, to your important relationships and to your longevity. Your deliberate self-talk and imagination is instrumental to change.

Daily and Periodic Rituals

It is helpful to consciously develop rituals that will serve you well. Rituals for your success that will become just as natural as showering and brushing your teeth.

As previously intimated, your top priorities might ideally be, paying attention to (i) maximizing wellbeing and (ii) doing things you love. In practice, there will probably be some things that you are not keen to do but are important to your success. The ability to keep moving forward towards worthwhile goals is what makes the difference and what separates the champions from the also-rans. This can involve self-discipline, but may be more a matter of installing good habits that are conducive to achieving our goals, and could also involve enlisting the support of others.

It's really important to start off each new and precious day in the right way, that is, with the right rituals for you. Sometimes the first hour after arising in the morning is referred to as the golden hour. With reference to the "Be-Do-Have Map" below, generally our lives can be summarized into the three interrelated areas illustrated, and either *consciously* or by *default* or a mixture of the two:

Be (Wellbeing and Presence): The starting point in this Map is to "Be" which as depicted below is related to our State of Being. We are better off living from a calm heart, (with brainwave frequency at the lower alpha or even theta states), as opposed to a busy and stressed head or mind, (with brainwaves in the beta state).

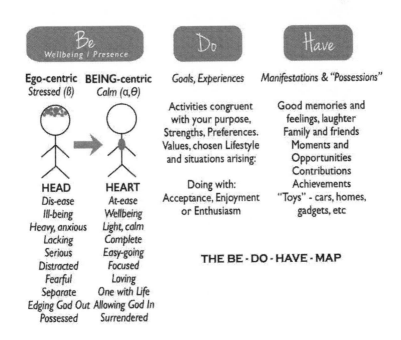

Be	Do	Have
Wellbeing / Presence		

Ego-centric	BEING-centric	Goals, Experiences	Manifestations & "Possessions"
Stressed (ß)	Calm (α,θ)		

Activities congruent with your purpose, Strengths, Preferences. Values, chosen Lifestyle and situations arising:

Good memories and feelings, laughter
Family and friends
Moments and Opportunities
Contributions

HEAD	HEART
Dis-ease	At-ease
Ill-being	Wellbeing
Heavy, anxious	Light, calm
Lacking	Complete
Serious	Easy-going
Distracted	Focused
Fearful	Loving
Separate	One with Life
Edging God Out	Allowing God In
Possessed	Surrendered

Doing with: Acceptance, Enjoyment or Enthusiasm

Achievements
"Toys" - cars, homes, gadgets, etc

THE BE - DO - HAVE - MAP

We have a thought for virtually every heartbeat during a typical day, and our minds are busy day and night even when we sleep. That's a lot of thinking and not always productive. Indeed, a high percentage of our thoughts are negative arising from our fearful egos and this tends to cause a certain level of background anxiety. This tendency is not surprising given that, as mentioned before, our lives are potentially fragile and of course limited in terms of lifespan.

Living from our divine forever-Being rather than separation is the best antidote that we have and interestingly this is synonymous with wellbeing.

Daily rituals that maximize *wellbeing and presence* can include:
- *Relaxation* to alpha or theta state followed by mind-set enhancing applications such as meditation, hypnosis, guided visualization, affirmation and neuro-linguistic programming. Regular "body scans" assist in relaxation and mind detoxification.
- *Mindfulness: Savoring every moment* in acceptance, enjoyment or enthusiasm: living in a state of aware presence
- *Fitness program* commensurate with your health and your fitness aspirations. Options include working out at a gym, exercising at home, and walking or running

In addition, it's important to pay close attention to your *diet,* (including hydration and moderate "juicing"), and the *quality* as well as duration of your *sleep.* If convenient, and you can afford it, a weekly massage, for example, every Friday lunchtime to usher in the weekend can be beneficial too. All of the above will help to provide you with energy and zest for life.

It is fundamentally important to note that our rituals for wellbeing generally involve taking *attention* away from the background scripts of our busy conditioned minds, and typically to our bodies, even during our daily activities. The resulting peace *from* mind tends to make us feel better and may also give rise to creative flashes of insight and intuition. Indeed, our very life *is* what we pay attention to, and maintaining a positive mood requires that we guard against unsolicited negative thoughts through *attention-management!*

Some useful supporting habits that help reinforce the shift from "Ego-centric" to "Being-centric" involve our habitual self-talk as we respond to daily events in our lives:
- **I'm still, here:** A reminder to be still, and present in the here and now directly. Look! Listen! Or indirectly: e.g. body scan, and follow your breath to *switch attention away from the mind!*

- **I'm still here:** Whatever happens, your essence and awareness is still here - losing an arm, leg, etc. would not affect your awareness that's been with you since you were born

- **I don't mind what happens:** A reminder to surrender and let go, resist nothing; what you resist persists, and whatever you are attached to possesses you; you are still free to change things

- **No problems *now*:** Problems are painful imaginations about *past and future* made by the fearful ego mind - you can deal with anything that comes up right *now*. Reframe and simply recognize things to attend to at the appropriate time which *would* be now in the case of a physical emergency. Write lists to relieve your mind of the need to recall.

- **I always cope in the now:** You know that <u>you have *always* coped</u> and you always will. It's not what actually happens, or will happen, but your fearful thoughts and stories that disturb your peace of mind

- **I am the master of my mind:** You manage your ego and learn to divert attention away from your mind to your body and breath, allowing higher intelligence to operate within you; be motivated by love and desire for good things not fearful reaction. Don't let any thoughts disturb you, get present! And love what-is as far as you are able.

Note that your *Quality of Life* depends on your internal and external environments. In planning your days, ensure that you spend time in environments conducive to your wellbeing.

Goals and Experiences: Now, wouldn't it be wonderful if operating from a springboard of energetic wellbeing, we could spend our days doing exactly what we want, love and enjoy? Well, this is where it's so important to choose our goals and purposes wisely and clearly. As we have already covered, and are emphasizing, there are three areas where many of us need to focus our attention and therefore set goals accordingly.

1. Wellbeing and presence – relaxation and renewal, preparation, *self-mastery* enabling you to operate from strength

2. Doing things that you love and are important to you – taking action, living your life and purpose; having a clear vision and mission

3. Generating passive income – freeing up your time, energy and passions, funding your lifestyle and enabling you to make a difference in the world

In developing the self-mastery needed to support your wellbeing and presence, it's important to identify and align with your *strengths, preferences and values.*

Now, although repetition will tend to strengthen your skill in anything, you will have some salient or *signature strengths* which you may or may not be aware of and possibly even misguided about. In order to ensure that you are developing the right strengths, you may find it helpful to take some credible self-evaluations such as Kolbe conative strengths assessment (www.kolbe.com), or the *VIA Character Strength* survey, (www.viacharacter.org). Having identified or confirmed your key strengths, which practices or experiences would develop them further to a laser light focus? Ideally you would be employing your strengths from a calm state of wellbeing and in a state of flow, maximizing unique contributions in your chosen pursuit or field.

Preferences refers to psychological and lifestyle as well as moment to moment preferences, and not a license to indulge in unhealthy temptations or habits! Certain of your psychological preferences are revealed through the Myer Briggs Test Instrument (MBTI) that you can take online. (A search engine inquiry would reveal various free and paid-for test opportunities).

Further information on *Values* is provided later in this chapter.

Having *clarified* your few top priority goals concisely in writing, daily rituals that maximize achievement of goals and experiences can include:

Goal Review: look at your few, written, compelling goals every day and possibly include them in a meditation or guided visualization or hypnotic script. (You can easily make up your own audios using voice recorder software if you wish).

Feel the feeling of your goals fulfilled. (That is to say you really have faith and believe in the outcome, (or something better). Your top goals need to include *daily* attention-management and self-mastery. Evaluate progress and next steps daily.

Time-blocking: whatever your chosen priority focus for today, you will probably need to spend several hours on it, and if practicable at times when you are typically more calm, alert and able to focus or concentrate. [And according to your practical situation and preferences – there is no need to follow prescriptions of some very well-established personal development practitioners to arise at 5am, or the almost contrary advice of another popular practitioner, to spend an extra hour asleep - unless these prescriptions really do suit you].

15-Minute Motivator – maintaining the crucially important discipline to succeed hugely: If you really do not feel like doing a necessary task or important step, perhaps due to a vague feeling of unpleasantness and the feeling that you'd rather be doing something more appealing, then really psyche yourself up and just give the task say 15 minutes of your time, (or even just 5 or 10 minutes), and see what happens. This may be the way to overcome your block. You could find yourself getting comfortable with the task, (not as bad as you thought), and find yourself making good progress. And, perhaps you may come up with some new insight or perspective that puts a different slant on things and makes things rather more delectable. If you do get off-track, consider what you are trying to achieve and renew your focus.

Repeat, repeat, repeat: Always remember that small steps, small directional changes, practiced consistently and faithfully can dramatically improve your outcomes or destination.

Achieving your goals should lead to good memories, moments and feelings, and laughter shared with your spouse, family, friends and acquaintances. And, fully engaged in the *game of life* irrespective of any afterlife beliefs, you can enjoy the fruits of your opportunities, contributions and achievements.

While there are many rituals that can be undertaken, you only need subscribe to a tailor made select few that suit you. Some rituals are best carried out daily and others may be say three times a week, weekly or monthly. And you need to develop the habit of reviewing your achievements and next steps on a regular, if not daily basis. Enlisting a friend in mutual no-cost peer coaching could be a good way to reinforce your habits and commitments.

Useful attention-management pointers include: (1) Am I present? (2) What is "The One Thing?" (3) Pareto 80/20 tendency (4) The Vital Few, (5) Scheduling and Time Blocking, (6) How am I feeling now? (7) Am I doing with enthusiasm and enjoyment? If not, why not? (8) Curiosity, (9) Open-mindedness, (10) Gratitude! Attention-management embraces mindfulness and meditation.

A key and primary *mind-set habit* to develop is to become fully present in the here and now. In the state of presence you are not trapped in day to day concerns about the past or future so you can choose to enjoy every moment. Just relax deeply and say to yourself, "I'm Still Here." This means, firstly, that you sense *stillness* in the here and now, you are relaxed, calm and free of any anxiety. This is a most important state that precious few people achieve on a relatively permanent basis.

Secondly, it means that whatever happens, (or is happening to you right now), your *essence* is unperturbed – no matter what happens to you you're still here. [Lose an arm your awareness is still here, lose a leg your awareness is still here, replace a body organ, your awareness is still here, take away thoughts (that come and go) and your awareness is still here. No matter what is taken away from you, can you see that your awareness that you have had from birth is still here?]. Realize then, that no event can upset your essence – only ego thoughts and emotions in reaction to the event can upset you, not the event itself. Resolve, decide that nothing will perturb your inner peace and use whatever method you are familiar with to become present now, thereby detaching or *switching your attention* from reactionary states to the peace of now.

If it helps, should you feel uncomfortable or overwhelmed from external events, throw an imaginary, fully protective thick, dense shield of impenetrable light around you, so that nothing can affect you while you see that *you're still* here, unaffected by externals; then regain your inner strength, calm and invincible composure. Train yourself to accept any negativity without getting caught up in it and go into solution mode; this may require some days of incubation and consultation before effective solutions emerge. Realize deeply that (i) there is no problem while living literally in the now; and that (ii) you will always cope in any future moment or now ... as you always have done.

Pay attention to forever-Being or *Big Mind*. You do this indirectly by shifting your attention from *ego* or little *mind* to your breath or body in a way that is familiar and comfortable to you. You are not your body, but the *animating presence*. This has been called "the light of the world."

Stop and recognize any painful time-dependent illusions passing through your mind; you can replace illusions with conscious thoughts, beliefs and self-talk that serve you. Furthermore you can adopt an attitude of loving everyone and everything; living in joy; dropping attachments, neediness, clinging. Surrender wholeheartedly to, indeed love and be grateful for, what-is. Get out of the imprisoning JAR of Judgment, Attachment and Resistance. These are all important spiritual habits to develop in support of being fully present for (real) life rather than lost in, and a victim of, undesirable **temporary** thought-emotion patterns.

As you go about your days, an attitude of **acceptance** and non-resistance to what-is, coupled with an attitude of **gratitude** will give you a lot of immunity against negative reactions. Mind-generated and time-based, *"negativity-ego-resistance"* are an interconnected trio that underpin painful emotions. A general **letting-go** will help prevent any negativity to stick and keep those associated painful feelings at bay. Try to respond from love and **compassion** rather than fear, yet work to change or remove yourself from any unacceptable situations arising. Try to make forgiveness of yourselves and others a given, so unnecessary. Since negative mind chatter is effectively involuntary, unconscious self-talk, try to relax, refocus attention, and, if it feels appropriate, counter the situation calmly with deliberate, conscious positive self-talk.

You may say, I do have a problem now. Well, whatever your life situation, try to remember that even that worst of fears, your death, is only death of your human form, not your essence. If you don't believe this, then perhaps nothing really matters anyway, and your life's purpose remains a mystery at best and a complete waste of time at worst! (The better option is to revel in the mystery!) Perhaps you say that you have a huge bill to pay and it's worrying you. Well, worrying is your choice, you don't have to worry, just schedule the issue, or if really necessary, deal with it immediately from a state of calm presence. You're still here aren't you?

From a place of presence and wellbeing, say to yourself "I Am Joy," perhaps while picturing the Life Purpose Map from Chapter 8 in your mind, and *knowing* that when you finally learn to get out of your own way, disquieting thoughts and emotions will give way to the joy of forever-Being. [Joy In, Joy Out – JIJO! You can choose to breathe in and out to this].

The link between joy and gratitude was discussed in Chapter 10. As previously mentioned, you can be grateful for your parents or caregivers who fed and clothed you for free; your education that may have been free; opportunities and valued acquisitions leading you up to the present day; Planet Earth and this amazing Universe, the air that you breathe, mighty oceans, mountains, galaxies and sunsets; a roof over your head; running water and electricity courtesy of your ancestors; and particularly the good things you can recall from the last day or so. Take nothing for granted! You can also maintain a gratitude journal.

Operating from the state of presence or forever-Being, you live naturally from joy, using your mind consciously to create what you want from your imagination. You can create in the state of flow.

Imagination

The art of imagination is very wide. Any question, any desire or dream enlists the imagination. Examining involuntary automatic thoughts, or deliberately and consciously thinking, enlists the imagination.

Practical uses of the imagination for realizing "impossible" dreams include:

1. Preview of your future through running mental movies every day
2. Assuming the *feeling* of the wish fulfilled – emotional engagement
3. Celebrating your dreams having already come true

Whereas *habits* of thought, feeling and behavior are automated programs that do not require conscious effort on your part, conscious and repetitive use of the imagination enables you to change your habits to meet your dreams and specific goals.

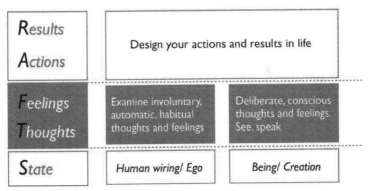

When you employ your imagination consciously, the future does not equal the past. Some people are naturally imaginative, it's a natural part of who they are, while others find that they have to be more deliberate and exercise self-discipline.

Imagination can *become* an important habit, for example as in deliberate, repeated visualization of certain images as part of a daily ritual. Imagination can also be held as a *value* that we use, or aspire to use, on a regular basis in creating our lives and mastering ourselves and our destiny.

Imagination is affected by our habits and values. Indeed, imagination tends to expand when fuelled by motivating values/needs, reframed beliefs and supportive habits or rituals that propel us in the desired direction. On the other hand, both *limiting habits and beliefs* act as a constraint on imagination. Fortunately, we can exercise our imagination in determining which habits to pursue, strengthen or drop, as well as to examine the solidity and efficacy of our beliefs and values.

It's no wonder that Einstein stated that imagination is more important than knowledge with his discovery that energy, mass and the speed of light are connected by the so beautifully elegant equation e=mc². And, the whole of Buddhism came about as a result of one man, Siddhartha, meditating under a Bodhi tree and using his imagination to understand the true nature of reality.

It is best to exercise one's imagination in a clear, calm, still and relaxed inner state. ["Be still and know I am God."] With reference to the 5I Map below, this may help you to open your *imagination* to connection with the formless *Infinite* and aid your *intuitions*. Through exercising your imagination, the formless can move into the world of form. Perhaps this is why "Neville," the popular 19th Century author, referred to imagination as "the Christ within."

THE IIIII (5I) MAP — IMAGINATION AND TRANSFORMATION FROM FORMLESS TO FORM

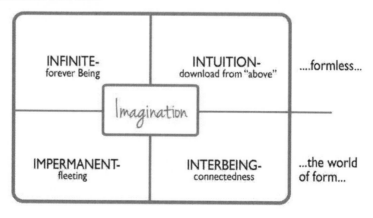

Physical creations, like the chair you're sitting on, or the book in your hands for example, are both *impermanent* and *inter-being* at the same time, as life continually unfolds. [The notion of inter-being was discussed in the Introduction]. Note too, that your creative thoughts and ideas are impermanent forms, so it is important to capture them before they are forgotten, so that they are put to good use, if and when a suitable opportunity arises.

Seeing back to our Source and Oneness is more a product of our imagination than knowledge – see the Introduction for the discourse concerning *who we are*. And freeing ourselves from fear – phew!! – covered in Chapter 7, is mostly a result of our imagination rather than knowledge. Again, in Chapter 8, examining the roots of love – *joy, contribution and do-no-harm* arose from imagination/ intuition. The subject of *Adventures* in terms of *life design* covered in Chapter 9 is all about using our imagination in *deciding* what ventures to embark upon and in invoking motivating emotions of excitement.

You *must* live the life that you have imagined! That's just how life works and so long as your imaginations are consistent with natural laws of the universe. The trick is to make your habits work for you and to develop your imagination so that you can challenge beliefs and see new possibilities for creating.

Creation = Habits ± Imagination

If you feel so inclined, you can put down your imaginations in a journal or dream or goal book. And, your deliberate self-talk and expectations should be in accordance with your imagination and vision. This will impact your behaviors and results positively towards the desired direction. *Every* thought that you have is creative, if only to stimulate emotions in your body, and of course these emotional stirrings lead to moods and actions. As noted earlier, we are creating through the mechanism of thought with virtually every heartbeat. [This is based on scientists reckoning that we have about 60,000 thoughts per day which if compared to around 100,000 heartbeats per day may result in one thought per heartbeat (or two) on average during the day].

How do you want to show-up in this world? Design it!

In Chapter 9 we provided a number of quotes in connection with our life's purpose, and our outer purpose is a natural outflow of our inner purpose. We quoted Eckhart Tolle suggesting that once we are in touch with our inner purpose, then external manifestations are things that we choose to engage in from a state of play rather than seriousness. In accordance with the Life Purpose Map, (see Chapter 8), contribution or service through giving back or paying forward, in short co-creation, is a necessary factor in living from the joy of being. And, while we will set intentions and follow up with action, we do it without attachment to the results and outcomes. We adopt the stance of spiritual masters in the expression "I don't mind what happens." So, with that firmly in mind you can choose to live in the manner of your choosing, (while adhering to the Golden Rule of "do unto others as you would have them do unto you").

In deciding how you want to show up in the world, you can adopt a simple categorization such as the 3M's: Mind-set and Moments as the main foci with Money as a supporting or maintenance factor rather than an end in itself. (That doesn't mean forget about money completely though because you need to ensure sufficient passive income to live the life that you choose and you need to manage your resources effectively). Or you may choose to use the more conventional "Wheel of Life" themes for life-planning that may include career, finances, relationships, health and wellbeing, self-image, etc.

Just to get you started, and this is a very personal matter, here are a few things you might want to consider:
- Where do you live? (E.g.: somewhere a bit exotic: start with a luxury apartment, for example, near the sea and consider upgrading to similar villa if family situation warrants)
- Where do you visit/ holiday? (E.g.: somewhere exotic. Consider history, culture, leisure, climate and quality of the natural and built environment).
- What do you drive? (E.g.: drive an open-roofed red sports car)
- What sort of clothes do you wear? (E.g.: look amazing and attractive, no matter your age)

- What is your skin like? (E.g.: get a nice tan; don't overdo it and protect yourself!)
- What is your partner like? (E.g.: get an amazingly attractive partner that supports your lifestyle perfectly)

Now, it's alright to desire nice things so long as you're not attached to them. And, so long as you adhere to the adage "everything in moderation," you should not suffer adverse consequences too much! The moment, journey and direction is what's important.

Love *what-is*! God is in everything!! Go where there is love ... where there is laughter ... where there is acceptance!!! (Or create it). And, if you're in a new environment just act as if you belong.

The World is your playground – it "belongs" to you (and everyone else if they but realize it); it's that same recognition that you are amazing, awesome, unique – you are indeed a unique part of the Universe and one consciousness.

Values

We are often extolled to live life according to our values. Why? Because living by our values and what we stand for makes us authentic, and can provide the daily moment by moment lens through which we perceive and interpret life.

If you have defined your values in the past, now may be a good time to re-appraise them. If you have never seriously contemplated your values, now would be a good time to start. If you do decide to live according to certain considered values, just make sure that you are really comfortable with them, which also means that considerable care is needed in defining or uncovering them. Note that in challenging circumstances, you will tend to respond or react according to your default values whatever they are. Indeed, crises may reveal your true values, and a crisis might also be the time to slow down and consider your values carefully to determine how you will respond most appropriately.

First decide, or at least contemplate, that you don't actually *need* anything other than a roof over your head, some clothing suitable for your environment and adequate food and drink to sustain your life. You may say, OK but I do need love. Well, believe, no, know that your Creator has already placed a fountain of love and joy in your heart and that when you give it away you will feel all the love that you could ever need. Here are some general pointers that you may wish to consider:

1. Don't shrink back from life – live it to the full
2. Life is love – family, significant other, friends, others
3. Live from true self – in the present, in acceptance, managing your ego wisely
4. Live to give without expecting any return
5. Enjoy every moment
6. Make adventure a primary value – live!

Values should tend to be expansive rather than constricting - for example, telling yourself that everything must be done right first time can be a recipe for failure – yes, it may apply to already perfected recipes or processes but that attitude never helped anyone to walk or ride a bicycle or to make a spectacular invention such as the first light bulb or airplane.

Now if you know your values and are truly living by them, that's great! If not, then you can decide to live your life more consciously which really means more happily by design, following your heart. It doesn't mean living your life on the hamster wheel trying to please or impress others. It may mean some willing sacrifices and inner work for a better future.

A word of warning in discovering your values as a reminder to yourself of what's important in life. They must be right for you, so require some deep thought and reflection. By way of example, I do not think that I would have settled on the FLAGS values, if I had carried out a typical "select your values from this list" exercise. While this can certainly be a useful starting point, and one is normally instructed to place these values in a priority order, you may have to ask yourself again and again and again what you really, really want. And, this may change as you go through the various phases of your life.

Now, your values in-use are the filter through which you both see the world, and decide how you will express yourself in the world. Beware though, that if you are aspiring to new values that are not yet habitual, old habits may draw you back to your old default mode!

Expression

There's a saying that "if you are easy on yourself, life is hard on you but if you are hard on yourself, life is easy on you." Well you don't necessarily have to be hard on yourself but if you have disciplined yourself to work on your habits, imagination and values then you will be in a better place to master your destiny and live the life of your dreams. In so doing, you will express your unique talents to the world in a way that is fulfilling for you and for the benefit of all.

Of course, the key change that is needed is the shift of consciousness from head to heart, from ego to forever-Being. Then many thoughts, feelings and behaviors will change automatically without a great deal of effort on your part as you participate in life in a more relaxed yet purposeful fashion. And, part of that will be a deep understanding of what's really important. You no longer need to anxiously follow society's norms or worry about the opinions of others.

Life is, and is intended to be, an exciting adventure; don't sleepwalk to your deathbed – live!! Express yourself! And, since you get what you pay attention to, it's good to invest in big dreams so long as these include for your wellbeing and joy. To paraphrase Gandhi, "your life is your message." Here are some things to consider in developing fruitful and meaningful self-expression:

- Consistently apply daily and other periodic rituals that support your growth, including attention-management, presence, awareness, relaxation and gratitude; exercise, sleep and diet routines
- Focus on the vital few and say no to the rest
- Make a difference
- Question your beliefs, stories and excuses
- Love your goals and any calling without attachment; enjoy the process, this step, the journey

- Be fearless by unblocking, surrendering to the joy of forever-Being – dropping all that is not you, your persona and personal baggage
- You are here to express not impress
- Avoid comparisons with others and "keeping up with the Joneses"
- De-clutter physically, mentally, emotionally & spiritually
- Lighten up, you're not going to be around as a human for long!
- Stay calm and present as often as possible; and,
- Live as forever-Being!

In summary, *renew your mind* as advised in at least one great religious book and focus on clear goals that support wellbeing and joy. Living out of Presence, (all-that-is), you create what-is (through habits, imagination and inspired action), and love what-is (Gratitude). Your creations may involve deep change.

As you go about your life, keep in mind that each living thing on this planet at this very moment represents the pinnacle, the *forefront* of existence in advance of everything that went before, through the amazing creations of our ancestors.

So realize that you are now at the forefront of all creation on Planet Earth! Who knows, perhaps your ancestors are relying on you. In any case, that doesn't necessarily need to concern you, this is your life and your destiny. Your past that has fully gone already does not equal your future and acknowledge that you are riding the current wave of creation in *every* new and fresh moment.

Expression is, can only be, right now this moment. Your amazing life is now. *Awaken* (to self-mastery) and (then) *achieve* (greatly). What is important is the step that you are taking now to achieve your current goals, *with* faith, *without* attachment. You have seen through the unnecessary suffering of mind, the need to break through limiting beliefs, and the need to commit to a clear destiny forged in moments of stillness. And, in so doing you will be contributing your unique gifts to the world. Enjoy the journey while being at *one with life*.

Above all, relax, *let go* fully, and don't fall into the trap of "I'll be happy when ..!"

Afterword

There seems to be way too much suffering going on in the world today. Life forms that "did not ask to be born," appear, suffer and die – what a tragedy this seems to us at the level of the human mind or little mind. Within the bigger picture and seen from the overall ongoing process of creation this is simply life playing out. We don't question the wisdom of nature in the forests, for example, where birth, death and renewal are ever present factors of life.

As humans we tend to take on an identity from our *limited* perspective, *separate* from the whole of which we are in fact a part, and take things way too seriously. Yet, life is full of paradox and while we needn't be so serious, as we have pointed out, you are truly on the current exciting wave of fresh creation so do take care to make the most of this one, short, unique and precious human adventure on Planet Earth.

Being present now, and *free of* the anxieties that come from psychological suffering allied to our imprisoning JAR (Judgments, Attachments, Resistance), to our limited sense of self, and detached from habitual thoughts and fears, we can be in touch with forever-Being. And in touch with forever-Being, which can only happen in the present moment, we can sense calm, a peaceful stillness, free of the main cause of suffering – our otherwise turbulent minds of self-protection. In *awakening* to forever-Being, we shift from *conditioned unconsciousness* to *non-conditioned consciousness.* Our thoughts and feelings are then fresh and creative, free of anxieties.

As the old adage says, "energy flows where attention goes." In the end, we can view life simply as 'attention-management' – wherever your attention is, *is* where you are, and accounts for the way that you feel. As humans we desire to *feel good* and to continually manifest *results* consistent with that. With reference to the RAFTS Map introduced in Chapter 1, results that arise from *awakened action* will be good for us and others. Our attention needs to be on the good, on *adventures of the heart,* inspired by joy as we open to the flow of life. We advocate using the primary Maps RAFTS, FLAGS and HIVE introduced in Part 1, Part 2 and Part 3 of this book respectively. The individual elements of the RAFTS and FLAGS Maps are interrelated:

- *Thought* (letting go of thought-identification and opening to the *flow)*
  Leads to <u>Freedom</u> *from* "monkey-mind" *to* wellbeing and joy

- *Feeling* (joy, flow and creative energy, unburdened by ego-self)
  Leads to <u>Love</u>, appreciation and zest for life

- *Action* (fuelled by love, appreciation and heart qualities)
  Leads to **Adventure**, and results, indulging the senses

- *Results* (rewards, creations and contribution of unique gifts/ talents)
  Leads to <u>Gratitude</u> for creations and contributions

- <u>State</u> of Awareness as forever-Being

  Leads to <u>Service</u>, living from Source/ Creator

Using the **HIVE** Map, you can develop your **H**abits, **I**magination and **V**alues to **E**xpress yourself wisely, uniquely and effectively in the world at large. Perhaps, one day, all humanity will awaken to their true selves and the madness in humanity will disappear. No more wars, manipulation, corruption and abuse. And, then people will be able to lead more sane and fulfilling lives. Until then, you have a great opportunity to live your best life right <u>now</u>, *training yourself to maintain attention on peace, love, joy and gratitude;* surrendered to the sunshine of Source; playing your part fearlessly, lovingly on the current wave of creation, fully engaged in this wonderful Game of Life before handing the mantle to the next generation.

Acknowledgements and Thanks!

Writing this book has been quite a solitary exercise, albeit for the most part an enjoyable one, sitting in picturesque cafes in Thailand sipping coffee. Yet, *producing and marketing* a book is another matter and inevitably involves participation of a number of people.

Thanks to Michael Buldoc and to Gwion Jacob Miles who introduced me to expertise in book publishing, editorial and graphic design. Special thanks to Rachel Turton who took my internal pictorial concepts and re-created them in spectacular fashion and devoted her substantial creative skills to the book cover design. Thanks to Ian Barnes who provided proofreading and suggestions on content, and to Jeff Williams for suggestions on publishing.

Thanks to Cloris Kylie, and to Stephanie Gunning and Peter Rubie of Lincoln Books, USA for comment on an earlier version of the book.

Thanks to Danny Speight and to Peter Culpan for assistance and advice concerning book printing and distribution in Thailand.

A big thanks to my parents, in Tonbridge, Kent, the Garden of England, always a great inspiration, and without whom this book would not have been written.

Last but not least, thanks to Michael Dobie in Indonesia who provided me with opportunities for writing and publishing *articles* as a prelude to preparing this book. (Articles for "Up.Date" magazine, a periodical produced by the British Chamber of Commerce in Indonesia and the Jakarta Post newspaper).

51962825R00114

Made in the USA
Columbia, SC
24 February 2019